AS MAINE WENT

AS MAINE WENT

Governor Paul LePage and the Tea Party Takeover of Maine

MIKE TIPPING

TILBURY HOUSE
PUBLISHERS

THOMASTON, MAINE

Tilbury House, Publishers
12 Starr St.
Thomaston, Maine 04861
800-582-1899 · www.tilburyhouse.com

Design by Lynda Chilton
BooksDesigned.com

Copyright © Michael Tipping
Library of Congress Control Number 2014022107
Paperback ISBN 978-0-88448-358-8
eBook ISBN 978-0-88448-359-5

Cover image: Governor Paul LePage speaks at a news conference to announce
new cabinet nominations, January 7, 2011, at the State House in Augusta, ME.
(AP Photo/Robert F. Bukaty)

Library of Congress Cataloging-in-Publication Data

Tipping, Mike.
  As Maine went : governor Paul Lepage and the Tea Party takeover of Maine
/ by Mike Tipping.
      pages cm
1. Maine--Politics and government. 2. Local government--Maine. 3. Lepage,
Paul. 4. Governors--Maine. 5. Tea Party movement--Maine. I. Title.
  JK2816.T56 2014
  324.9741'044--dc23
                        2014022107

Contents

For Alistair and Brennan

Introduction

It has been almost four years since November 2010, when a host of grassroots conservative candidates won local, state, and federal elections across the United States in an unambiguous sign of strength for the new Tea Party movement. Over the intervening years, barrels of ink have been spilled and millions of pixels darkened with debate about what the Tea Party is and how this right-wing force and the politicians it has helped to elect will influence the country.

Maine offers a unique case study of the effects of Tea Party governance. In 2010 the state's moderate to progressive voters split their votes between the Democratic nominee and her chief independent competitor in a three-way general election. This allowed the Republican nominee, Paul LePage, to win election with just 38 percent of the popular vote, largely as a result of the strength of his grassroots Tea Party support. LePage is without question the most conservative and controversial governor in modern Maine history. His rise signaled the end of a hundred years of moderate New England–style Republicanism in the state and a sharp break with the party of politicians like Margaret Chase Smith, Bill Cohen, and Olympia Snowe. In its place, LePage created a new Maine conservative coalition, one based on hard-right economic and social views and primed for political combat rather than legislative compromise.

The 2010 election also installed Republican majorities in both houses of the Maine legislature for the first time in decades, many of the new lawmakers having likewise been elected with Tea Party support. For two years LePage and his legislative allies had control of all the levers of state government and free rein to enact their agenda.

In 2012, as the nation reelected President Barack Obama, Maine's electorate changed gears and again elected a Democratic majority in both houses of the legislature. This lessened LePage's ability to pass new policy, but the resulting political dynamic played well to his predilection for combat and his obvious fondness for the role of a figure of opposition. The second half of LePage's term has therefore offered a demonstration of how a chief executive with a Tea Party ideology and disposition deals with a competing branch of government controlled by the other party.

Throughout his time in office, Governor LePage has made statements and taken actions that have attracted national attention and alienated moderate voters.

He has attacked the NAACP as a "special interest" and told them to "kiss my ass." He has joked that the worst his lax policies on toxic chemicals in consumer products would do is cause women to "grow little beards." He accused a state senator who opposed his tax policies of "giving it to the people without using Vaseline." He has claimed, completely without evidence, that an active wind turbine was fake and run by "a little electric motor," and that fully 47 percent of able-bodied Maine residents are refusing to work.

While these and other outbursts may have brought national ridicule and hurt his standing with moderate voters, they have done little to erode his overall level of support and may actually have helped him among his base of Republicans and conservative independents. The negative attention his antics have attracted has allowed him to paint himself as a victim of a biased media. Many of his Tea Party supporters see the controversies as sure signs that he must be shaking things up in Augusta.

LePage's approval ratings throughout his time in office have hovered around 38 percent, the same percentage of the vote he received in 2010.

While parts of the Tea Party may have withered since the 2010 election, with rallies attracting fewer participants, blogs and web forums going dormant, and grassroots energy giving way to control by national, corporate-funded Tea Party organizations, the movement has grown in the power it holds over elected officials in the Republican Party and in government. Politicians on the right, including almost all the leading Republican presidential contenders for 2016, have adopted an extreme, uncompromising approach to policy and governance, and the ideals and emotions of the movement have become the dominant ethos of the Republican Party.

National and Maine polls have also continued to show large numbers of Republicans and conservative independents identifying themselves as supporters of the Tea Party, at levels that are little changed since 2010.

With another multicandidate election for Maine governor slated for November 2014, including a run by the same independent candidate, Eliot Cutler, who drew more than a third of the vote in 2010, LePage's low approval numbers may not prevent him from winning another term as governor. Much will depend on how the broader electorate perceives his record and how motivated his base is to reconstitute the Tea Party surge that helped him win four years ago.

A great deal of the attention Paul LePage has received during his time in public life has focused on his bombastic and often offensive statements. This book is intended as a means of acknowledging but looking past those outbursts and examining his record as a politician and governor in a more comprehensive way. It is an attempt to answer questions about how he gained support and won election, how he has governed, the issues he has pursued in office, and the consequences of the policies he has enacted. It's also an attempt to examine the motivations and background of some of LePage's strongest supporters, who have maintained their ideological alliance with the man they see as one of their own even as many of his policies seem to have had detrimental personal and economic effects on their lives.

LePage's governorship–especially the interplay between his grassroots base, the corporate interests that have backed his rise and helped to dictate his policies, and his own often combative personality–offers important insights into the kind of government that may result wherever Tea Party-backed individuals are elected. It provides a case study of what happens when politicians who are radically opposed even to some of the most basic functions of government come to power and what might happen nationally if their movement gains more influence or if a Tea Party candidate is elected president.

chapter 1 The Watchmen

At 8 a.m. on February 4, 2013, a signal crackled to life from the WXME radio tower in Aroostook County, about a mile and a half from the Canadian border. The broadcast went out locally on the AM band as well as the station's online stream. The signal was picked up from the Internet and rebroadcast through a network of low-power FM repeaters maintained by volunteers willing to skirt the edges of FCC regulations in towns across Maine. Listeners tuning in that morning were greeted first with a medley of patriotic and religious songs and then by the voices of Jack McCarthy and Steve Martin, hosts of the Aroostook Watchmen radio show.

McCarthy and Martin are two men with a cause. They believe they have access to truths that few others know or want to hear, primarily that the American government is illegitimate and that the shadowy cabal of elites who control it are preparing for a war on the American people. The 9/11 attacks, the Boston bombing, most mass shootings, and a wide range of other events generally attributed to terrorists and criminals are actually false-flag operations perpetrated by the American government against its own people as part of a ramp-up to a final reckoning, according to the hosts. The Watchmen, who consider themselves "Sovereign Citizens" outside government control, feel it's their responsibility to reveal these conspiracies and to help wrest back control of the country from the usurpers. Their program is broadcast six days a week.

This particular Monday morning, the Watchmen discussed new evidence that they said proved the Sandy Hook school shooting was a false-flag operation made possible through government mind control.

They warned that Jewish Senators Diane Feinstein, Chuck Schumer, and Joe Lieberman were attempting to disarm the patriots of America so that they could begin their "holocaust against America's Christian population." They also had something more locally relevant to talk about: McCarthy's hour-and-a-half meeting, two days earlier, with Maine Governor Paul LePage.

The meeting with the governor had taken place two days after McCarthy and a group of fellow conspiracy theorists calling themselves the Constitutional Coalition held a press conference at the State House. They stood behind a podium in the Hall of Flags (just outside LePage's suite of offices) and announced that the president of the Maine Senate, the speaker of the Maine House of Representatives, and Governor LePage had all violated their oaths and should be removed from office. The group explained that they had submitted a set of "remonstrances" to all three government officials on January 14 accusing them of acting unlawfully and had received no reply. Under their unique interpretation of the Maine Constitution, this meant that all three politicians must surrender their elected offices. The men were there to announce their intention to enforce that judgment.

One of the participants, Constitutional Coalition leader Wayne Leach, made reference to the American Revolution and declared that "hopefully this remonstrance, which uses words, will be sufficient. The weapons, I hope, will not be used."

Article 1, Section 15, of the Maine Constitution states that "the people have a right at all times in an orderly and peaceable manner to assemble to consult upon the common good, to give instructions to their representatives, and to request, of either department of the government by petition or remonstrance, redress of their wrongs and grievances." Most would interpret this passage as a general guarantee of freedom of speech and petition, but Constitutional Coalition members seized upon the language to mean that they could submit a "remonstrance" in order to "give instructions to their representatives" that would be binding on all government officeholders simply through the fact of its submission.

The remonstrances the group submitted to LePage and the legislature accused Maine's government of being unlawful, of having illegally accepted and used unconstitutional currency (anything other than gold and silver), and of coordinating with UNESCO, UNICEF, NATO, and the UN to deprive Americans of their property rights. An e-mail sent to the governor's office by Constitutional Coalition spokesperson Phil Merletti, along with the remonstrance document, declared that legislators who had violated their oaths in this way were committing treason and domestic terrorism. He suggested that they listen to the Aroostook Watchmen radio show for more information.

The staff at the house and senate leadership offices responded to the Constitutional Coalition's submissions as they do to most correspondence that tilts toward the crankish–they accepted the documents politely, then filed them away to be ignored. Governor LePage's staff acted much the same, just as they had with previous communications from members of the coalition.

LePage's staff, including executive assistant Micki Muller, who reviews the governor's e-mails, had previously shunted aside requests from Merletti to meet with LePage regarding a bill to reform the Land Use Regulatory Committee, which Merletti claimed was a plot by radical environmentalists and "a vicious act against the citizen's unalienable [sic] rights of Maine people." They similarly ignored a proposal from Wayne Leach that the state stop using the illegitimate U.S. dollar and create its own new currency called "MaineBucks."

This time, however, word of the remonstrances and the press conference made it past the executive office gatekeepers and to the attention of Governor LePage himself. Rather than ignoring the submission and its radical claims, LePage called Merletti at home at 9 a.m. the next morning in order to set up a meeting for that Saturday with members of the Constitutional Coalition. According to a note that Merletti sent to his e-mail list later that day and that was forwarded to LePage and members of his staff, the governor was angry that he hadn't heard about the remonstrances earlier, and during the call he pledged to fire any staffers found to have been keeping the information from him.

Later that day, LePage's director of constituent services, Patricia Condon, asked the Executive Protection Unit of the Maine State Police to run background checks on four members of the Constitutional Coalition: Merletti, McCarthy, Leach, and another man named Gary Smart.

As McCarthy later revealed in his conversation with Martin on the Aroostook Watchmen radio show, the meeting that weekend covered a wide range of topics. The members of the Constitutional Coalition informed LePage that the United Nations and the Rockefellers were plotting to take over Maine's North Woods. They discussed the illegitimacy of the U.S. Department of Education and argued that the state should refuse to accept federal education funding. (According to McCarthy, the governor "hung his head and said you're right" in response.) They also informed LePage that U.S. paper currency is unlawful. ("He was mesmerized by that," said McCarthy.)

During the meeting, the Watchmen presented LePage with a copy of the 2012 Maine Criminal Justice Academy training manual, which instructs law enforcement officers on how to handle encounters with members of the Sovereign Citizen movement. The manual states that "the FBI considers the Sovereign movement one of the nation's top domestic terrorist threats." The Sovereign Citizens in the room took issue with that information and asked LePage to remove it from state law enforcement training materials.

The manual is correct in its assessment. The same rejection of government authority that prompted the Constitutional Coalition to file their remonstrances often brings Sovereign Citizens into conflict with police and government officials. Many of the crimes they commit based on their beliefs are of the white-collar variety, including bank fraud, filing false liens, money laundering, illegal firearms sales, tax violations, and the manufacture of false documents. When they are confronted over these violations by police officers, whom they view as agents of a fraudulent government, however, the situations sometimes escalate to violence.

According to the Federal Bureau of Investigation, Sovereign Citizen extremists have killed at least six law enforcement officers in the

United States since 2000. In one such incident in 2010, two Sovereign Citizens were pulled over by local police in Arkansas in a routine traffic stop. They pulled out an AK-47, killed the two officers, and fled the scene. They were eventually killed in a Walmart parking lot after a shootout that injured two more police officers.

In addition to these more random acts of violence, some Sovereign Citizens have also planned significant antigovernment terrorist attacks. One of the most well-known Sovereigns is Terry Nichols, who helped to plan the bombing of the Alfred P. Murrah Federal Building in downtown Oklahoma City in 1995, killing 168 people and injuring hundreds more.

On one episode of the Aroostook Watchmen show, McCarthy spoke about having met and worked with Schaeffer Cox, the founder of the Alaska Peacemakers Militia, a Sovereign Citizen group. In January 2013, Cox was sentenced to twenty-six years in prison for conspiring to murder federal and state government officials, including judges and law enforcement agents, and for stockpiling illegal weapons and explosives.

This history of violence, much of which is detailed in the law enforcement manual that was handed to Governor LePage, casts a troubling light on some of the topics of conversation at the State House meeting that day, and some of LePage's responses.

When discussing Senate President Justin Alfond and House Speaker Mark Eves, both Democrats, McCarthy apparently claimed that they were guilty of "high treason" and noted that the penalty for treason hadn't changed in a hundred years.

"I never said it, but the governor said it. I never opened my mouth and said the word," explained McCarthy. "The governor looked at us and looked at his buddy and said, 'They're talking about hanging them.'" (The "buddy" was apparently a member of LePage's legal staff.)

According to McCarthy, at another point in the conversation, when discussing federal funding, LePage said, "If I go any further with this bill, with this refusal to accept federal money, they will surround this building and kill me."

"I believe he thinks that literally, absolutely literally. I said if you call we will come and defend you," said McCarthy on his show.

McCarthy's description of LePage's participation and remarks might be dismissed as simply an unfortunate series of miscommunications and exaggerations of the actions of a governor just trying to appease some constituents and supporters without really understanding who he was talking to or what he was talking about. The fact that the meeting was far from a one-off event makes this less likely, however. The Watchmen describe–and e-mails and documents obtained from LePage's staff through Maine's Freedom of Access laws confirm–at least eight meetings over a period of nine months in 2013, almost all more than an hour in duration and some lasting almost three hours.

During these regular meetings, according to the participants, the governor was "educated" by a series of "experts" brought in by the Constitutional Coalition on a number of their conspiracy theories. LePage also made a series of promises to the Watchmen that he would assist them in pressing their cases of treason against Eves and Alfond and in pursuing their wider antigovernment aims.

At the next meeting with the governor, on February 16, the lead "expert" in attendance was Michael Coffman, a conspiracy theorist, author, and lecturer who believes that the United Nations is attempting to seize Americans' private property and usher in an oppressive one-world government through the use of local sustainability initiatives, smart growth plans, and by pushing the "myth" of global warming.

Two days later, a discussion was held on the Aroostook Watchmen show featuring Coffman, McCarthy, Merletti, Leach, conservative activist Roger Ek, and former State Representative Henry Joy (perhaps best known for submitting a bill to allow northern Maine to secede from the rest of the state), all of whom attended the meeting. According to these participants, topics of conversation with the governor included the coming collapse of society, the illegality of income taxes, the sale of the American people as chattel to the International Monetary Fund, the buying up of ammo by the Department of Homeland Security as part of the government's preparation for the coming war against American citizens, and the UN's plan to depopulate the entire northern tier of Maine.

"I was very pleased with the governor," said Coffman. "You know anybody can say anything with any kind of accent, but he seemed like he was genuinely concerned and agreed with us on almost every point."

This wasn't the last time that LePage and Coffman collaborated. At the meeting, LePage agreed to attend a talk by Coffman being held two months later at Lake Region High School in Naples. According to an article in the *Bridgton News* describing the event, the governor attended, gave opening remarks, and then stood by as Coffman spoke to the audience not just about his UN conspiracy theories but also about a plot he claimed was underway to force the teaching of socialism in public schools and his belief that "Barack Obama's presidency is part of a plan by the Islamic Brotherhood to turn America into an Islamic controlled nation."

LePage met with the Sovereign Citizen group for a third time in April. As the meeting approached, LePage's staff exchanged e-mails about who would have to attend along with the governor, with none of them seeming to want to be in the room. "There is no question but that it be staffed," wrote executive assistant Micki Mullen. LePage's chief of staff John McGough "pulled rank" and refused. Eventually, LePage's director of boards and commissions, Michael Hersey, agreed to attend, as members of the legal staff weren't available.

Less documentation exists for the contents of the April meeting (and the Watchmen didn't discuss it on their show), but it apparently focused on the issue of wind power. The Constitutional Coalition members believe that large-scale wind power development is not just undesirable but part of a conspiracy to deprive them of their land and freedom.

A little more than a week after the meeting, while speaking to the Skowhegan Chamber of Commerce, LePage blasted wind power and made a strange claim about one wind turbine in particular:

"Now, to add insult to injury, the University of Maine, Presque Isle–anybody here been up there to see that damn windmill in the back yard?" asked LePage. "Guess what, if it's not blowing wind outside and they have somebody visiting the campus, they have a little electric motor that turns the blades. I'm serious. They have an electric motor so that they can show people wind power works. Unbelievable. And that's the government that you have here in the state of Maine."

The governor was later forced to recant his accusation after his remarks made national news. He tweeted, "It was not my intention to misspeak about UMPIs windmill, but I admit I had misinformation." He did not reveal the source of the false conspiracy theory.

On May 29 the Constitutional Coalition members held a conference call with LePage and began to make some more specific requests of the governor. In a letter that Merletti sent to LePage before the meeting, the Sovereign Citizen leader asserted a constitutional right of Mainers to carry concealed weapons without a permit and asked that LePage stand up to the "anti-gun factions, supported by Socialist and Communist leaning defenders of the global left," and bring an emergency bill to preserve this right. He also asked LePage to use the power of his office to "summon Sheriff Liberty" (Sheriff Randall Liberty serves Kennebec County, including Augusta, the state capital) to hear their complaints that the speaker of the house and president of the senate were committing treason. (Sovereign Citizens believe that the only legitimate law enforcement officer is an elected sheriff.) Merletti warned in his letter to LePage that if his group continued to be ignored by the legislature, "we will be left with the 1776 or 1865 option. In the pursuit of liberty there is no extremism."

Governor LePage apparently promised to summon the sheriff, and on July 3 the Constitutional Coalition members and the governor met with Liberty in a boardroom in the State House. The sheriff had the time wrong initially, but after LePage called him on his cell phone, he arrived within five minutes.

"It was a monumental meeting. I think that meeting will definitely go down in history," said Merletti two days later on the Aroostook Watchmen show.

In the meeting, LePage asked Liberty to visit Maine Attorney General Janet Mills and ask Mills (a Democrat elected by the legislature) to meet with the Constitutional Coalition to reconsider the group's demands. Wayne Leach had previously been rebuffed when he visited the attorney general's office on behalf of the coalition and asked them to arrest Speaker Eves and President Alfond.

"The governor stepped in at this point in time and he says 'What you have to understand is that these gentlemen are telling you that they want you to follow through on this because this is a constitutional issue that they violated not only one time but three times,'" explained Merletti on the show. "That just put me back in my chair that the governor would say such a thing."

In that meeting, the participants also again discussed the Maine Criminal Justice Academy's Sovereign Citizen curriculum, and they asked about the role of the governor and the sheriff in the event of an attempt by the federal government, through the Federal Emergency Management Agency, to institute martial law and bring in Russian troops to invade the state.

"They're going to have to get by me first," replied LePage, according to Merletti.

In an interview, Sheriff Liberty confirmed the timing and topics of discussion of the meeting and said he attempted to steer the conversation away from "that conspiracy theory stuff" as much as possible. Following the meeting, he complied with the governor's request and visited the offices of the attorney general and county district attorney to ask them to hear the Constitutionalists' case.

LePage would later echo some of the Sovereign Citizens' rhetoric about sheriffs when he stood next to the Cobscook Bay State Park boat launch on October 17 and declared that he wouldn't allow the federal government to close the launch as part of the government shutdown (which had actually already ended eight hours earlier).

"The sheriff is the chief law enforcement officer in the state of Maine and I will authorize him to keep this place open," said LePage.

At the time, the remark puzzled political observers. Those without a background in Sovereign Citizen conspiracy theories brushed it off as a simple misstatement by LePage.

On August 7, the members of the Constitutional Coalition held yet another meeting with Governor LePage, this time to share new information about their attempts to prosecute Eves and Alfond. They also brought in Lise McLain, a fellow Sovereign Citizen who had done some of the research that informed the movement's theories about the illegitimacy of the government and the courts.

Despite Sheriff Liberty's intercession, the group's attempts to prod the attorney general into action had failed. They told the governor that their next plan was to open up a common-law court in order to try the two men. The state courts that currently existed were fraudulent, according to the Watchmen, because they practiced "admiralty law." This deception was revealed, they claimed, by the fact that the flags in the courtrooms had a gold fringe.

They also informed the governor of their recent meeting with the head of his administration's risk management department, whom they had asked to rescind the state insurance policies covering the house speaker and senate president.

According to a recap by McCarthy and Merletti on the Aroostook Watchmen show, the meeting went well and they were enthusiastic about the outcome, particularly because LePage had promised to make public his support for their theories.

"The public's not going to wake up with you and I standing on a street corner flapping our arms, but when the governor calls a press conference, they show up," said McCarthy. "So he has said he will call a press conference at which we will be featured."

"That will be more than interesting," agreed Merletti. "The governor has lost a lot of his followers over the years, but they're going to wake up to see that this man is honest."

Soon after this meeting, a Freedom of Access request for the documents that have informed much of this report was filed, alerting the governor's staff that word of the meetings had spread. Sometime before the governor's next meeting with the Constitutionalists, LePage's legal staff presented him with a five-page memo arguing that the Sovereign Citizens were misinterpreting the law. They wrote that the right of remonstrance "does not include and has never included any rights of citizens to compel legislation or compel the government to act in any certain way." In short, they finally explained to LePage the sheer ridiculousness of the basic premise of the conversations the governor had been having with the group for the prior eight months.

On September 14, 2013, Governor LePage, accompanied by staff lawyer Hancock Fenton, met again with the Watchmen and discussed this legal opinion. It would be the group's last meeting with the governor. The press conference was canceled. Although the Constitutionalists were disappointed by this outcome, they say they're still grateful to LePage for all the time and support he gave to their cause.

"I'm not writing him off," said McCarthy when asked in October about his opinion of the governor. "I'm very disappointed in some of the positions that he reneged on but in many respects he's done more for this state than any governor in the last thirty years."

Even without the governor's help, McCarthy and his fellow Watchmen haven't given up their pursuit of Alfond and Eves. They are currently attempting to impel a grand jury to indict the two men for their supposed crimes against the Constitution.

Nor should the Watchmen be disappointed with the amount of time and attention the governor paid to them. Before his lawyers finally convinced him to stop, LePage had engaged more fully in their conspiracy theories than he had in many of his official responsibilities. In fact, he had spent far more time meeting with the Constitutionalists than he had spent meeting with the house speaker and senate president they were attempting to prosecute.

At the same time that LePage called Merletti and first proposed a meeting in January 2013, the governor was publicly refusing to meet with Alfond and Eves, whom he hadn't communicated with personally since their election three months earlier, despite their repeated requests. Earlier that month, LePage had declined to perform the governor's usual role in presenting his biennial budget to the legislature, instead leaving the task to his finance commissioner.

A little more than a week before his first meeting with the Sovereign Citizens, LePage had also stormed out of a meeting with three independent legislators. According to media reports, after the lawmakers questioned his proposal to cut off municipal revenue sharing the governor pounded the table, swore at them, called them idiots, and stormed out, slamming the door behind him.

In May the governor, fed up with his interactions with Democrats in the legislature, announced that he would be moving his offices out of the State House completely. (He later changed his mind.)

The meetings also represented far more time than LePage had spent talking to the press. Already known for refusing interviews, in June 2013 LePage announced that no member of his administration would be allowed to talk to three of Maine's largest newspapers after the *Portland Press Herald, Kennebec Journal,* and *Morning Sentinel* published their investigative report on corporate influence within his Department of Environmental Protection.

Also that spring, LePage put in place a new policy to severely restrict the access of legislative committees to members of his administration, one that continued in force throughout the rest of the session. In September, shortly after his last meeting with the Sovereign Citizens, the governor announced that he would be taking the unprecedented step of refusing to submit a supplemental budget proposal for the next year, leaving the legislature to figure things out on their own.

Given this well-documented refusal by LePage to extend any courtesy to those he felt were wasting his time or working against his interests, the amount of attention and deference he paid to the members of the Constitutional Coalition (despite attempts by his staff to prevent it) makes it clear that he felt that meeting with the group was a worthy use of his time and the resources of his office. So do the statements he made and actions he took to promote their causes.

Why would a governor value the support of such a group when an association with their violent, antigovernment, anti-Semitic conspiracy theories could damage him politically? How could he think that discussing how best to arrest and execute his political opponents with a group of Sovereign Citizen extremists was a good idea?

Two answers seem most likely: The first is that he may have bought into many of the Sovereign Citizens' claims, at least until his legal staff set him straight. This is certainly what the Watchmen believe and is reinforced by his willingness to repeat some of their rhetoric in public. The other possibility may be that LePage simply wished to flatter this group with his time and attention because, despite their extremism, they are a crucial part of the electoral coalition that helped him to gain his office and may be useful to his reelection in 2014.

The Aroostook Watchmen show isn't just a voice in the wilderness. It has hosted a who's who of the conservative far right in Maine, including leading Christian conservative activists, the heads of the various Tea Party groups, state legislators, members of LePage's administration, presidential candidate Ron Paul, and, during the 2010 primary, LePage himself. LePage was one of three candidates who sought the support of the show's listeners and the endorsement of hosts Martin and McCarthy. He even participated in a live debate on the program opposite fellow Republican primary candidate William Beardsley.

Members of the Constitutional Coalition and their supporters are well connected within the larger conservative and Tea Party establishment in Maine. They have taken leadership roles in a number of local and statewide Tea Party groups, and some have sat on the Republican State Committee.

Aroostook Watchmen host Steve Martin worked closely with LePage campaign staffer Cynthia Rosen and a group of LePage supporters and Tea Party members to rewrite the state GOP platform in 2010. Some of its planks, including a mandate that the party "prohibit any participation in efforts to create a one world government," echo Sovereign Citizen rhetoric.

During the Republican primary campaign for governor in 2010, Martin and McCarthy hosted a regular conference call that served to unite the disparate Maine Tea Party groups toward a common purpose and, eventually, toward the election of Paul LePage. They played a significant role in organizing and energizing the army of grassroots volunteers that helped him to win first the Republican primary and then the general election.

Even at that time, however, Martin and McCarthy were seen as extremists and as representing a potential threat to LePage's campaign if they were tied too closely to the candidate. Other Republicans publicly warned him to stay away from, as one conservative columnist put it, "pirate radio stations and people who believe in black helicopters."

The reasons Governor LePage devoted so much time and energy to the Constitutionalists and what he thought about their theories may never be fully revealed, in part because key documents that might have provided insight into this question seem to have gone missing. According to numerous on-air statements by the Watchmen, LePage took copious notes at several of their meetings. McCarthy even remarked once about how his daughter, who was in attendance, imitated the governor by scribbling on her own pad of paper. These notes were not provided in reply to a Freedom of Access inquiry despite being specifically requested, and LePage's legal staff claimed to have no knowledge of their existence.

The idea that LePage may simply have been humoring the Watchmen as a way to secure their continued political support is one that came up often in discussions on their radio show, but they dismissed it as unlikely based on the number and length of the meetings they had with the governor and his continued apparent interest in their theories and support for their cause.

"We started working with him in January or February, we've met with him on average once a month," explained Merletti on a show in August. "The least amount of time that he's given us is an hour and a half. We've gone within a few minutes of three hours. You just don't give that kind of time to people that don't have credibility."

chapter 2 The 2010 Campaign

On a Sunday evening in January 2010, Paul LePage, the mayor of Waterville and general manager of Marden's Surplus and Salvage, a chain of fourteen discount retail stores, logged on to the Internet forum hosted at AsMaineGoes.com. Using the pseudonym ForThePeople, he composed a series of posts about the Republican primary race for Maine governor in which he was a candidate. In these posts he took advantage of the forum's anonymity policies to describe his qualifications in the third person.

"Beat the Elite vote for the person who truly wants to represent the Maine People, not the entrenched special interest," wrote LePage in one such post. "Vote LePage for Governor, he has a proven track record in government, business, many non-profit organizations and the life experience to make a difference for Maine People. Many candidates have business or government experience but lack both."

The online handle used by LePage wasn't chosen lightly. It spoke to his campaign's theme of aggressive, conservative populism, an approach that would position him perfectly to take advantage of the national Tea Party wave and harness a new grassroots movement building in Maine. He would continue to use the pseudonym for the next few months, pretending to be an outside voice defending his record as mayor, bragging about how much financial assistance he had provided for his family, and supporting his positions on various issues. He also repeatedly and anonymously rebuked other users for doubting his electoral chances.

Before the year was over, LePage would be proven right. He and his grassroots supporters would "beat the elite," just as he had promised in his posts. Not only would he win the seven-way Republican primary by a wide margin, but he would win the five-candidate general election as well. In the process he would sweep away much of the political establishment in Maine and make room for a new order.

The conservative wave that swept over the 2010 election also carried GOP majorities to power in the Maine House of Representatives and Senate. For the first time in more than thirty years, Republicans found themselves in complete control of Maine's state government and in a position to shift the state toward their conservative goals. The choices that LePage and his legislative allies would subsequently make to strip away environmental regulations, slash public assistance and health-care programs, and cut income and estate taxes, largely to the benefit of Maine's wealthiest residents, would eventually affect the lives of hundreds of thousands of Mainers.

As Maine Goes, the conservative web forum in which LePage made his anonymous posts (here for the first time attributed to the governor's personal account), takes its name from the old political slogan "As Maine goes, so goes the nation," which hailed Maine as a national bellwether. Until the 1950s, Maine held its elections in September of each evenly numbered year, two months prior to the rest of the nation. In the generations before reliable public opinion polling, the vote for Maine's governor (which took place every two years before Ed Muskie, governor from 1955 to 1958, convinced the state legislature to lengthen the term of the governor succeeding him to four years) sometimes provided the first real indication of the national mood and served as a predictor of which party would win the presidency. The national political parties often spent outsized resources in the state in an attempt to win local elections and create a sense of broader momentum.

Maine's reputation as a political oracle ended dramatically in 1936. In that year, Republicans swept the state's September elections and the national Republican Party pointed to the result as a sign that President Franklin Delano Roosevelt's popularity was waning. Despite the early results in Maine, Roosevelt won a crushing victory over Alf Landon in the presidential vote two months later. Only Maine and Vermont gave their electoral votes to Landon, prompting Roosevelt's campaign manager to quip, "As Maine goes, so goes Vermont." Maine would again have close elections and would sometimes be contested ground in presidential contests, but it would never again be seen as a crucial bellwether in a national election. In modern politics, the phrase might instead begin, "As Ohio goes . . . ."

With the election of LePage and his Republican majorities in 2010, however, Maine again found itself in the vanguard of a political movement, with the potential to become either a positive advertisement or a cautionary tale for the nation regarding the effects of Tea Party control.

The fires of political change that LePage helped to stoke were first sparked in places like the Herbert Sargent Community Center in Old Town, a central Maine town known mostly for hosting a struggling paper mill and for making high-quality canoes. There, LePage spoke to a Tea Party rally the same weekend he wrote those online comments.

The crowd of around 200 people at the event had come together over a shared distrust of the new president in Washington and his ideas for health-care reform. They had begun organizing themselves through local meetings and through online social-networking sites with names like Maine Patriots and The Maine Refounders. More recently, they had begun to hold larger rallies like this one. Also recently, large numbers of them had begun to publicly express their support for LePage.

"It's a pleasure to be back to speak to the Tea Party group and today, more than I ever, I will say I need your help," said LePage, beginning his 25-minute address to the crowd. "This week has been a pretty tough week. Never in my life would I have thought that someone that you supported for two terms and was her campaign chair in one county would throw you under the bus. And I'll tell you, it's time to beat the elite.

"It's time that we the people, the hard-working people of Maine take over our government," LePage went on. "We want it back. The entrenched establishment is going to be facing the Maine people in

June and we're going to tell the entrenched establishment, it's time to go. So we together can send a strong message to the political career-minded politicians and say it's time to go home."

With his comment about being thrown under the bus, LePage was referring to the entry of Steve Abbott, chief of staff for Senator Susan Collins, into the race for governor that Tuesday. LePage had twice served as Kennebec County campaign chair for Collins, a moderate Republican, and had hoped for her support despite his differences with the senator in ideology and tone. With Abbott's entry it became obvious that he wouldn't be getting it (she would choose not to endorse anyone in the primary), and from that point forward, LePage's language about the need to oust the entrenched establishment would intensify.

Abbott's entry rounded out the ballot for the Republican primary, raising the number of candidates seeking the nomination to seven, each with a unique background and representing a different segment of the Maine Republican coalition.

Abbott was seen as the establishment choice, and LePage's Tea Party allies would mock him as "Steve Machine." He had never held elected office, but was a part of Collins's inner circle, and his announcement was met with quick endorsements from elected officials and Republican Party stalwarts. According to Abbott's campaign staff, they originally attempted to court the Tea Party, but as LePage locked up movement support, Abbott's invitations to Tea Party rallies and events dwindled and then ceased.

Candidate William Beardsley, the former president of Husson University in Bangor, posed perhaps the greatest threat to LePage's hold on Tea Party support. He was the most socially conservative of the seven candidates and located his core support among the religious right. He was also, perhaps to his detriment, more congenial by nature than the mayor of Waterville and less willing or able to exude angry indignation in his public appearances. LePage's anger better fit the Tea Party mood.

Another candidate, Matt Jacobson, was a businessman and president of an organization created to bring businesses to Maine.

Jacobson constructed his electoral argument on his ability to attract companies and create jobs. It was a powerful argument, but he was unable to pair it with strong fundraising or significant grassroots support and would end up finishing in last place.

Peter Mills, a state senator from Cornish, was the only primary candidate other than LePage to have held elected office. A moderate, Mills had voted in favor of same-sex marriage and had been the only Republican senator to vote for a 2009 tax reform proposal that his fellow Republicans had labeled a tax hike. The new law faced a repeal referendum as part of the same election as the primary, shining a spotlight on Mills's vote.

Part of a political family (which also includes his sister Janet, a Democrat and Maine's current attorney general), Mills had also run for the Republican nomination for governor in 2006. In that primary he lost to the more conservative Chandler Woodcock, who went on to lose to Democratic incumbent John Baldacci in a multicandidate general election.

One of Mills's best arguments in the primary was that he was the strongest candidate for the general election, and that if he rather than Woodcock had been the nominee in 2006, Republicans might already control the Blaine House. Within the primary field, Mills was the lone defender of the old-school moderate Republicanism for which Maine had historically been known. He was also the only Republican candidate to accept public financing for his campaign through Maine's Clean Elections Act.

Businessman Les Otten was well known for being a ski resort magnate and a former co-owner of the Boston Red Sox. As a candidate, he focused squarely on the issue of jobs and his background as an entrepreneur. He announced for governor early and ran hard, airing television ads far before his opponents and eventually spending $2.5 million on the race, most of it his own money. He came to be viewed as the main threat by some of his primary opponents, and he led in the only public, independent poll of the race.

Missteps by Otten, including the plagiarizing of campaign materials and the revelation that he had previously contributed to

Democratic candidates, were highlighted by opposing campaigns looking to blunt his monetary advantage. He would eventually place a distant second behind LePage.

Millionaire investor Bruce Poliquin rounded out the field and, like Otten, largely self-funded his campaign, spending nearly $800,000. At times he attempted to court the Tea Party vote, but he couldn't seem to convince them of his authenticity or overcome their distrust of his record, which included previous support for gun control measures and environmental organizations. Poliquin wore his ambition on his sleeve and pursued the nomination with a single-minded forcefulness that distanced him from his fellow candidates and may have turned off Republican voters. Maine Public Radio reporter A. J. Higgins likened his presence at primary debates to "a skunk at a picnic," noting in a column at the time that the other Republican candidates shared "a unique distaste for Poliquin."

A late TV attack ad run by Poliquin against Otten under the grammatically incorrect but memorable title "Les Otten, Less Jobs" ended up damaging both of their well-financed campaigns and may have helped to pave the way for LePage's victory.

Unlike many of the candidates, Poliquin's politicking didn't end in 2010. He has continued to pursue elected office with the same energy he displayed in the primary campaign, but also with a new appreciation for the power of the Tea Party. After placing far back in the 2010 primary, he vigorously campaigned for LePage, was appointed by the Republican legislature to serve a term as state treasurer, and unsuccessfully pursued the Republican nomination for the U.S. Senate in 2012. He is now running for Congress in Maine's Second District, having won the Republican primary with Tea Party support. In all of his subsequent campaigns, he has attempted to align himself closely with the governor and his electorally powerful far-right base.

The seven-way 2010 gubernatorial primary race for governor was loud, expensive, and hard-fought, with millions spent on advertising and little consensus throughout on which campaigns had an electoral advantage. Many state political experts predicted an Otten or Abbott victory until the end. In the final count, however, LePage won the contest going away. He garnered 37 percent of the vote among the 131,000 Mainers who voted in the primary, almost double the turnout of the last contested GOP gubernatorial primary. Otten was second with 17 percent of the vote, followed by Mills with 15 percent, Abbott with 13 percent, Beardsley with 9 percent, Poliquin with 5 percent, and Jacobson with 3 percent.

No one was more surprised by these results than the Mills campaign. Mills had hired the husband-and-wife data and polling team of Stephanie Dunn and Mark Smith and, in consultation with the state senator's brother, Paul Mills, a noted state historian, they developed a detailed model of the electorate based on decades' worth of past election results. They updated it throughout the race with information from the campaign's voter identification efforts and a series of internal statewide polls. But the 2010 election turned out to be very different from the previous elections on which they had based their model, and their projections severely underestimated the Tea Party vote.

In their last poll before the election, the Mills campaign found their candidate in the lead with 25 percent of the vote, ahead of Otten, in second place, by eight percentage points. LePage was in fourth place with 11 percent.

The poll included other results that should have given them pause, however. Even among their targeted, traditional Republican voters, a strong plurality said the Tea Party movement was a good thing for the party and, even just a few days before the election, 26 percent of those they identified as likely voters refused to say for whom they would vote.

It didn't take long on election night for Mills's advisors to realize their mistake. When the results from Portland, Maine's largest city and a liberal bastion, showed LePage winning by a wide margin, they immediately realized how badly they had misjudged the electorate and how far the Maine Republican Party had shifted from its moderate roots.

"When we found out LePage won Portland, it was time to start drinking because we knew it was over," said Smith. "That was the first result that we got of the night and Peter called to concede at that point."

The other campaigns had a similar focus on likely voters and were similarly surprised by the scale of LePage's victory.

Some had a bit of advance notice. A few days before the primary, Otten's team had commissioned a poll surveying a much wider slice of the electorate and had found a high level of interest in the election and support for LePage among those they had thought were unlikely voters. They realized they were in trouble but didn't have enough time to react.

The Abbott campaign also sensed hints of LePage's momentum through their voter identification calls in the days before the vote.

"Our polling up until the last four weeks was good. We were in the race, we were on TV," said Abbott campaign political director Mark Ellis. "Then we started through our voter ID phone calls to see more and more people not saying who they were supporting. At that point, we kind of knew."

The first two vote tallies reported to the Abbott campaign that night were from York and Aroostook counties, at opposite ends of the state. When both tallies showed LePage far ahead, the Abbott campaign staff saw that the race was over and that something very unexpected had happened.

LePage and his campaign had seen and seized upon an opportunity that most of the other candidates had missed. His unique political attributes, his personal background, and his angry populist tone allowed him to take advantage of the political shift in a way no other candidate could. LePage was also willing to take big risks to further his campaign, risks that could easily have come back to burn him. He repeatedly resorted to a series of whopping lies on the stump and embraced individuals and groups on the fringes of the Tea Party movement with some truly repugnant views, including the Aroostook Watchmen. Because he was never seen as a front-runner, however, these weaknesses were never exploited by his opponents. They were too busy attacking each other, and, with few exceptions, the media also didn't begin to take real interest in his words and actions until after he had won the Republican primary.

According to LePage's chief political strategist, Brent Littlefield, LePage's opponents still haven't learned the lesson of his victory.

"I would argue that most people–especially other Republicans who were on the ballot in 2010–don't have a true understanding of what happened during that cycle," said Littlefield. "Some people, especially those on the far liberal side, might like to feel comforted in thinking that Paul LePage won because of some mystery movement. However, Paul LePage was chosen because he had a proven track record of business success, he has a dramatic life story that proves he wants to see others succeed, and Paul left a successful career to run for governor not because he wanted a title but because he cares about Maine people."

Littlefield is certainly right that it took more than just the votes of Tea Party members for LePage to win first the primary and then the general election, but Tea Party backing was key to his success. Tea Party supporters came to see LePage's campaign as part of their movement, and many of the Maine Tea Party's most active members logged off their message boards long enough to canvass their neighborhoods, register voters, and get them to the polls. The LePage campaign was able to get attendees at Tea Party rallies to leave with canvass sheets and spend their nights and weekends knocking on doors, advancing the kind of mainstream arguments that Littlefield touts in order to convince more moderate voters to back their more extreme candidate.

LePage was dramatically outspent during the election, but the currency he earned with the Tea Party ended up being much more valuable. As he noted in a post he wrote using the ForThePeople pseudonym three months before the election, "On June 8, I believe they count votes not money."

chapter 3 The Footsoldier

Who were these new political participants that boosted LePage to victory? Polling in Maine shows that supporters of the Tea Party movement are most likely to be male, middle-aged, married, and living in the central and northern parts of the state. They are less likely to be a member of a union than the population in general, and although around 60 percent count themselves as Republicans, another 30 percent consider themselves independents and 10 percent are Democrats.

Carter Jones, one of Governor Paul LePage's earliest and most dedicated campaign volunteers, is a good representative of this group. His background and the story of how he became involved in politics helps shed light on the movement as a whole. It also contains a number of parallels with LePage's own life story, which represented a key part of the governor's electoral message.

Jones works as a logger and lives with his wife and their children in the central Maine town of Aurora. His four sons range in age from ten to twenty. The oldest serves in the National Guard and hopes to go into security. The youngest attends the Airline School in Aurora, named for its proximity to "the Airline," a stretch of Route 9 between Bangor and Calais known for its hills and the logging trucks that go barreling over it at what might seem to an observer to be ludicrously dangerous speeds.

Jones's mother, who raised him and his four siblings by herself, worked at a sardine factory in Eastport, and Jones and his brothers and sister all worked hard jobs from an early age. His mom retrained when the plants began closing, becoming the first woman in Maine to graduate from vocational school as "one hell of a carpenter," according to her son. She worked for a furniture company in Amherst and received her pay in cash, under the table, so she could continue to collect public assistance. "She was basically institutionalized on it," said Jones.

The memory of his mother's reliance on state aid is a difficult one for Jones. He believes in hard work and self-reliance and is proud that his own family was recently able to buy their own health insurance. Throughout the campaign and LePage's first two years in office, his children relied on the state's Medicaid program, called Maine-Care, for coverage.

Jones's mother had a problem with alcohol, and her home wasn't a happy one. Jones's twin brother left home at the age of fifteen, and Jones followed a year later.

"I walked into the house one day and my mom was sitting there with a half gallon in one hand and a drink in the other," recalled Jones. "When I opened the door she looked at me and said, 'Where the hell you been?' I was just coming from work, you know. I was that age. I just turned around and walked out the door and that was it. I lived in a tar paper shack, finished graduating from high school, and went to work."

In many ways, Jones's upbringing mirrors that of Paul LePage, who also came from a broken and abusive family and found himself homeless on the streets of Lewiston at the age of twelve. LePage's background engendered in him a lifelong commitment to preventing domestic violence and a distrust (similar to Jones's) of public assistance programs, which he sees as creating a culture of dependency.

LePage talks often about his hardscrabble upbringing, sometimes somberly, sometimes with humor.

"Now, most of you know my background. If you don't, I was homeless, I come from a big family of eighteen kids and we were poor and I'm talking about dirt poor," LePage told a conservative women's group in 2013. "Back when I was about eight years old, I got a Christmas gift. It was a flashlight to go cut wood so we could heat the house. When I was nine years old, I got the battery."

Some of LePage's most thorough public recollections about his childhood came on the occasion of his first visit back to his hometown of Lewiston after becoming governor.

"Merci beaucoup, c'est avec plaisir de retourner à la ville de mes ans," said LePage, whose first language is French, to the crowd at the Lewiston Franco-American Heritage Center a few months after the election. He reminisced about growing up in the part of town known as Little Canada, named for the French-speaking immigrants who came from Quebec to work in the local mills. He talked about the tenement building where his family shared space with eleven others, together raising a total of eighty-three children. He also joked about the mean streak that he developed living on the streets.

"So I used to hide right here down the street in little alleys between buildings," said LePage, remembering a Halloween night when he was twelve. "We used to hide there and when little kids would come by we'd steal their candy. Isn't that awful? And now I'm governor of Maine."

LePage's difficult childhood and French ancestry have both been useful to him at points in his political career. The former has given him an aura of legitimacy possessed by few other politicians when discussing issues of poverty. Whenever he is accused of being unfair to the poor (an increasingly common occurrence throughout his time in office), he can trot out his personal history for refutation.

LePage's French ancestry gave him an entrée with a crucial voting bloc in Maine elections. Franco-American Mainers of Québécois or Acadian ancestry comprise a potent political force in Maine. They're concentrated in northern Maine and in a swath of mill towns and former mill towns running down the center of the state: Madawaska, Millinocket, Waterville, Lewiston, Biddeford, and others. One in four Mainers claims French or French-Canadian heritage.

During the last century, Franco-Americans formed much of the backbone of the Democratic Party in Maine, although their candidates often lost to Irish politicians in party nominations for top state offices. Only one Franco-American served as governor before

LePage–Democrat Alonzo Garcelon in 1878–and he was selected by the state legislature rather than publicly elected.

Mainers with French heritage are often Catholic and culturally conservative, but are usually supportive of labor unions and the economic policies of the Democratic Party. The St. John Valley in northern Maine, for example, has one of the highest Democratic registration advantages of any region in the country, something you might not expect based on the number of statues of the Virgin Mary dotting well-manicured lawns and the prevalence of gun-rack-equipped pickup trucks in the region.

In recent decades, Franco-Americans have become a crucial swing vote in state politics. The LePage campaign canvassed heavily in Lewiston, the second-largest city in Maine, and other historically Franco areas, also running radio ads and sending campaign mail in French. LePage made up ground in the city relative to previous Republicans and won a plurality of the vote there both in the 2010 Republican primary and in the general election.

It was LePage's heritage and reliance on the French language that also indebted the young future governor to the family of Olympia Snowe, Maine's long-serving centrist senator. After LePage left his abusive home, Olmpia Snowe's first husband, State Senator Peter Snowe, was one of several members of the local community who helped him find his way off the streets. According to LePage, Snowe convinced the powers that be at Husson College in Bangor to allow him to take the SATs in French in order to gain acceptance to the school. He went on to earn a degree in business administration and finance there while editing the school paper and serving as senior class president. He later earned an MBA from the University of Maine.

From this shared history, despite differences of ideology and tone, Olympia Snowe and LePage formed a political bond. She endorsed him in 2010, and he endorsed her in 2012 despite complaints from his Tea Party base. Although she left the U.S. Senate before the 2012 election in part because she felt politics had become too partisan, Snowe maintained her support for LePage and has helped to raise money for his reelection campaign.

Carter Jones had a similar experience with an early mentor, although not one as politically powerful as the Snowes. For him, it was a friend's mom, an English professor at the University of Maine at Orono, who stepped in to provide support and guidance when he left home. "I learned a lot from her about being patient and how important education was," said Jones.

It was education that first prompted Jones to become involved in politics, particularly the school-consolidation fight under Governor John Baldacci, LePage's immediate predecessor. Baldacci is a Democrat but pursued a number of conservative ideas during his eight years in office. His administration proposed reining in spending on education by mandating that local school districts consolidate in order to reduce overhead costs. He argued that Maine was far below the national norm when it came to students per district and had many more superintendents and school boards than its population could support (a criticism LePage continues to echo).

When legislation backed by Baldacci mandating that Maine's 290 districts consolidate into 80 was passed in 2007, there was immediate opposition, especially from rural areas of the state. The effects of the reform were felt far less in southern, more populous areas where larger districts were exempted, but residents in northern, western, and eastern coastal Maine were faced with the prospect of widely separated towns being lumped together under new regional administrative units. Residents of small towns feared a loss of local control and local identity, and the proposal inflamed geographic divisions that have long been a part of Maine politics.

This split between what's often called "the two Maines" is a defining feature of state politics. While a variety of historical, cultural, and economic trends have created a patchwork of political and demographic regions across the state, one of the most obvious divisions is between the more urban and suburban south, centered on Maine's largest city of Portland, and the more rural remainder of the state. Bitter feelings exist on both sides of the divide. Some in the more affluent south protest that they represent the state's economic engine, and that rural Maine leeches off their success. Some in the north claim that they represent the "real Maine" and that southern Mainers are unfairly interfering in their affairs, especially when it comes to issues of forestry, hunting, and land-use rights.

These issues and these cultural and political divisions were at the center of Jones's political awakening and would also play an important role in LePage's political rise.

Although Governor Baldacci's plan for schools passed in the state legislature, opponents of consolidation continued to fight for what they saw as the principle of local control. In 2008 they gathered more than 60,000 signatures opposing the law, enough to place a repeal referendum on the statewide ballot for the following November.

Consolidation opponents raised $66,697 for their campaign, mostly from rural town governments and individual donors. Baldacci's campaign to preserve the law raised more than seven times as much, mostly from large corporations, many with no real interest in consolidation but with business before the Baldacci administration. In the end, Baldacci and his allies won handily, with 59 percent of the statewide vote and larger margins in the south.

The referendum amplified the long-building phenomenon of rural political grievance, and many in central and northern Maine saw it as an example of big business and liberal, pro-government politicians working together to take away their rights. The dynamics of the fight certainly added to the sense of rural alienation that fed the growing Tea Party movement.

An anti-gay marriage referendum, also in 2009, and the vote on the tax reform proposal during the primary in 2010, provided further organizing mechanisms for social and fiscal conservatives. Together, these exercises in direct democracy helped to limber up some of the grassroots muscles that the Tea Party put to work in 2010.

Jones, offended by what he perceived as the heavy-handed way in which Governor Baldacci had approached the consolidation issue, looked around for a way that people could get more involved in the political process. He found a natural home in the nascent Tea Party movement and soon became one of its early leaders.

Jones remembers a meeting in Portland in the spring of 2009 as being especially important in the growth of the Tea Party movement. It came only a few months after CNBC Business News editor Rick Santelli first called for a tea party rally in Chicago to protest President Obama's economic policies, an event many point to as the founding moment for the Tea Party. The Portland meeting was convened by Pete Harring, a Republican organizer who refers to himself as "Pete the Carpenter" (in imitation of conservative activist and John McCain supporter Joe the Plumber) and had founded the state's leading Tea Party web forum. Twelve movement leaders gathered from across the state, some of them driving many hours from northern Maine. Realizing that they had started something with a great deal of potential, the attendees took turns stating their goals for the movement.

"I said my goal is to replace the governor with someone who would move us in a little better direction on education," said Jones. "The guys there, we all had basically the same idea, of working to replace the governor with somebody with some common sense."

This was a time when the Tea Party movement across the country was just beginning to find its feet and identify some common policy targets, including lower taxes, opposing the federal stimulus package, and stopping health-care reform. In Maine, in addition to supporting these national goals, Tea Party leaders embraced a practical, local, electoral focus right from the beginning. Specifically, they set their eyes on the Blaine House.

The group that Harring had brought together began to develop a strategy for electing a right-wing governor. They decided to focus on grassroots organizing in every corner of the state in order to create new, local Tea Party groups. They also prioritized having Tea Party members become involved in existing Republican organizations with the hope of influencing them or taking them over.

"I was kind of a strategist at the time," recalled Jones. "I said, look, we've got people from all over the state here, from north to south, east to west. Let's try to build some momentum and basically get into the party that we thought would be headed more in the direction that we wanted, which was the Republican Party."

They also planned for leaders in the various local groups to stay in touch through regular meetings and conference calls. There was neither a leadership hierarchy over the many clubs and organizations that would soon form nor a single accepted template for how they should function, but there was plenty of strategic coordination among a core group of activists.

Before the twelve attendees left that meeting in Portland, they made plans to research and evaluate the candidates for governor, find the one who best matched their view of the world, and use the grassroots power they were building across the state to make sure that person would be nominated and elected.

Despite their goals, many of these early members of the Tea Party movement felt that the organization should maintain a nonpartisan sheen. Some of the original organizers felt strongly enough about not being identified simply as Republican that they convinced Pete Harring to change the title of his website from Paint Maine Red to Maine Refounders. The site would become one of the best organizing tools for the fledgling movement, with regular blog posts and e-mail updates and more than a thousand members. It was rivaled in size and influence in the movement only by the Maine Patriots website and message board hosted by an activist named Amy Hale.

One of the Tea Party movement's great strengths at this time was that it was largely made up of people such as Jones who hadn't previously been politically involved. They had new energy, and the fact that they weren't deeply informed on political and policy details and instead spoke more about basic values was an advantage as they worked to spread their ideas.

"One thing that people need to understand about the Tea Party movement in Maine, and I'm talking just Maine, is that it was a group of people who basically had had enough, just regular everyday people who weren't up on politics or anything, and I think that's why it was so successful," said Jones. "I could go talk to my neighbor and say 'Jeez, it seems like we're in a mess with the debt and the deficit and more power being taken by the government' and almost everybody would agree with that.

"I think most people that I worked with at the beginning had that same thought process and feeling that 'if I went and talked to my neighbor, instead of having one vote, I'd have two.'"

Jones says things changed later, as more people with agendas joined the movement and as supporters of presidential candidate Ron Paul worked to fold elements of the Maine Tea Party into their campaign. But in the beginning it had the feel of an independent and organic uprising.

Much of the financial backing for Tea Party groups and activities nationally has come from a set of established conservative organizations, many of them with ties to right-wing oilmen David and Charles Koch. These organizations did provide materials and direction for some of the activities of the early Maine Tea Party movement, but Jones insists that the grassroots work they did was more homegrown sod than out-of-state Astroturf.

"Americans for Prosperity, for example, I don't know who funds them and I really don't care," said Jones, referring to an organization founded by the Koch brothers that has become a major part of the Tea Party ecosystem in Maine and across the country. "I don't believe groups in general were manipulated by Americans for Prosperity in Maine because most people who had stepped forward to lead these groups were people just like me."

That meeting of budding Tea Party leaders was also where Jones first heard the name Paul LePage, when Harring mentioned him as a likely contender for their electoral support. Soon after, he began to hear about the Waterville mayor regularly from fellow activists and then began to see him in person at Tea Party events. The first time he saw him speak was a rally in Etna-Dixmont, but Jones didn't offer his support or even speak to LePage then or at the next gathering where he saw the candidate, or at the next.

"I don't trust any politician, so I didn't trust a lot of what he was saying at first," said Jones.

The trust grew over time, however, as LePage continued to court the Tea Party and shape his message to fit the movement's ideals.

Jones also heard from Bruce Poliquin at many of these meetings, but quickly dismissed the millionaire investor as not ideologically pure enough for his tastes.

"I talked to him myself and I asked him, 'Are you willing to take federal money with strings attached?'" said Jones. "He answered yes and I told him right there, 'You're off the list.'"

By the fourth event in which he saw LePage in action, Jones had made up his mind. It was a meeting in Old Town of several hundred Tea Party supporters, and Jones had arrived early to help people sign up for the Tea Party e-mail list. He left his post by the door to approach Paul LePage and campaign staffer Jason Savage.

"I basically said 'I've been following you for a while, I like what you're saying,'" said Jones. "I told them I had done some research on how candidates in your situation win state elections, and I took out Sarah Palin's book. She gives all kinds of information in there on how she won that election and I highlighted it in the book and I give him the book and I said, 'Here's how you win.' We become pretty good friends after that."

Jones became a dedicated volunteer. He attended strategy meetings and became part of the campaign's inner circle. He continued to attend Tea Party events, but now also represented the LePage campaign and worked to recruit volunteers.

"I spent as much time as I possibly could. Any meetings that I heard of where we could be promoting Paul LePage, I was there," said Jones. "We covered some ground and spent some late nights."

He was also dogged in his online promotion of LePage, posting on Tea Party message boards and social media, signing up supporters to the candidate's Facebook page, and slowly creating a legion of networked fans of the mayor that he could call on to swamp online polls and flood newspaper comment sections.

LePage's online support was one of the few early, visible signs of the strength of his candidacy. While fund-raising totals and polling showed other candidates with the advantages, the size of LePage's social-media lists and the visible activism of his online fans hinted at the size and enthusiasm of the grassroots army he had begun to harness.

Not everyone in the campaign understood what was happening at first, and campaign chief of staff (and Waterville's police chief) John Morris didn't think initially that online campaigning would figure much into their strategy. But Jones, along with Savage, who had worked in IT for LePage at Marden's, convinced Morris that social media was an important investment, especially if they could turn online support into offline campaign activity.

"Even a guy like me in Aurora could really reach out all across the state," said Jones. "I was on every night. I'd come home from work and be eating my dinner and be missing a lot of time, sacrificing time with kids, but it was important to do that, to keep that momentum going and keep furthering our contacts and gaining members."

Perhaps most importantly, Jones also threw himself into old-fashioned shoe-leather campaigning. He spent every weekend knocking on doors, leading volunteer teams to canvass in towns and cities all over the state.

"Sarah Palin laid it right out in that book. That's the way to get voted is to go out to these areas in rural Maine," said Jones. "They trusted what we were saying because we're just like them. We're fishermen, we're loggers, we're construction workers, auto workers, mechanics, just regular guys out there on a Saturday. I'd tell them that I work in the woods five days a week from three in the morning to five at night, but I'm out here on a Saturday because that's how concerned I am for the direction for your kids. Our kids are in jeopardy."

Later, after winning the governorship in no small part because of the work of Jones and the volunteers Jones had recruited, LePage would send Jones another book, *Broke*, by Glenn Beck, signed by the governor-elect, by LePage's daughter Lauren (who also worked on the campaign), and by Olympia Snowe.

LePage also asked for Jones's resumé to consider him for a post in his new administration.

"I will look into it, at the moment I have no idea what is available, but I assure you if there is a job it will be yours," LePage wrote to Jones in an e-mail.

In the end, it didn't work out.

"He actually tried to put me on the board of education, because my concern is the kids," said Jones. "But that didn't happen because I have a pretty colorful past with the law. I'm no angel. I'm more of an angel now than I used to be, let's put it that way."

chapter 4
The 2010 General Election

As Paul LePage's campaign transitioned from the primary to the general election in June 2010, he faced two significant differences that would test his candidacy. First, the electorate he now had to contend with was very different from voters in the Republican primary, both in scale and composition. With a much larger and more moderate population to appeal to, his Tea Party base, no matter how active and engaged, would be less able to tip the scales in his favor.

Second, LePage suddenly faced a new level of scrutiny from the media, voters, and the campaigns and allies of his general-election opponents. Some of the same attributes and factors that had helped him in the primary wouldn't work as well in the context of a general election. These included his angry demeanor, his propensity to repeat anecdotes that were provably false, and some of the associations he had cultivated in order to build his Tea Party coalition and win the Republican primary.

These weaknesses were no surprise to those following the election. They had been noted publicly by supporters of other candidates.

"The problem with LePage is, in every debate he says things that are both stupid and factually wrong. He got away with it in a seven-way primary, but would not in a general election," lamented Republican lawyer Dan Billings, writing on As Maine Goes. "The Dems will eat LePage alive. He keeps using that line that it is illegal to dump a bottle of Poland Spring water in a Maine river. That's complete b.s."

Billings would later support LePage in the general election, serve as chief counsel for his administration, and be appointed by the governor to a judgeship, but during the primary campaign he was a consistent critic of LePage and the "crazies" who, he said, made up much of the core of the mayor's campaign.

"You want the votes of the crazies, but you need to keep them in the back room and out of the public eye," wrote Billings. "Not all LePage supporters are crazy. But some of his closest advisors are crazy. And he is openly courting the fringe."

Republican Matthew Gagnon is now director of digital strategy at the Republican Governors Association and is working to help LePage get reelected, but during the primary he had similar fears about LePage and stated them with specificity on his Pine Tree Politics blog.

"The biggest asset of Paul LePage's campaign for governor is himself and his supporters. The biggest enemy of Paul LePage's campaign for governor is himself and his supporters," wrote Gagnon on the day before the primary. "[T]here are supporters–a significant number of them–who are embarrassing their candidate and turning off voters by taking things a bit too far. The first large-scale example of this that we saw was what happened at the GOP convention with the school being trashed."

Gagnon was referring to an incident in which a group of Republican delegates from Knox County attending the May 2010 party convention in Portland ripped a poster on the history of the U.S. labor movement from the door of the classroom in King Middle School, in which they were holding their caucus, and replaced it with a bumper sticker reading "Working People Vote Republican." They also apparently went through the teacher's supplies and left him a note saying, "A Republican was here. What gives you the right to propagandize impressionable kids?" after finding copies of the U.S. Constitution that had been donated by the American Civil Liberties Union. The Maine GOP issued an official apology for the delegates' actions.

The events of the convention at the time constituted almost as much of a turning point for the Republican Party in Maine as did

LePage's primary win a month later, and both were orchestrated by the same group of Tea Party activists.

The convention adopted a new, extremely conservative party platform containing support for far-right fringe policies and references to conspiracy theories. It called for the elimination of the Department of Education and the Federal Reserve, demanded an investigation of "collusion between government and industry in the global warming myth," promoted the adoption of "Austrian Economics," called for the abrogation of the "UN Treaty on Rights of the Child," and proclaimed resistance to "efforts to create a one world government."

Billings, among other more-moderate Republicans, responded strongly to the content of the new platform, calling it "wack job pablum" and "nutcase stuff."

The drafters of the new platform included some of the same Knox County activists who were responsible for the classroom vandalism. One of their most prominent leaders, medical marijuana farmer and anti-vaccine activist Cynthia Rosen, was also one of Paul LePage's highest-profile Tea Party supporters.

Rosen saw the passage of the platform with a strong majority at the convention as a good sign for their movement and for the LePage campaign.

"It blew open the doors to an awareness of what existed that these people really had no clue about," said Rosen. "The powers that be didn't realize that there were so many people who were connected and communicating and actively working together across the state. Even a lot of folks who were involved in this grassroots movement going on didn't realize how many we were."

Like Carter Jones, Rosen was one of the twelve early Tea Party leaders who met at Pete Harring's house in Portland in 2009 and agreed on the goal of electing a conservative governor. Soon after, she began volunteering for LePage and using her Tea Party connections to build support for his candidacy.

"I gave up my whole frickin' life," said Rosen. "I began traveling around the state and really bringing Paul into these groups early, before the other guys were really getting there. Getting folks to look at him first seems to have made a very big difference."

In late 2009, Rosen's work as a grassroots organizer became official when she was hired as a LePage campaign staffer. Her employment didn't last long, however, ending in January 2010 when she wrote a controversial public letter attacking rival candidate Steve Abbott and Republican First District congressional candidate Dean Scontras in scathing terms. The paychecks from the campaign stopped coming, but Rosen remained a dedicated volunteer for LePage throughout the rest of the primary and general election campaign.

After LePage became governor, Rosen and her husband raised the money to buy a large sign reading "OPEN FOR BUSINESS," which LePage had the Department of Transportation install at Maine's border with New Hampshire.

Rosen and her associates could certainly be considered loose cannons, but she wasn't the most extreme of the Tea Party leaders that LePage courted. During the primary he seemed willing to become involved with just about anyone on the right who could bring along some votes, no matter how radical their politics. Gagnon specifically critized LePage for seeking the support of the Aroostook Watchmen, led by conspiracy theorist Steve Martin.

"LePage himself (or his campaign) can be blamed for some of this, because he has made no secret of trying to attract these people," said Gagnon. "He (and Bill Beardsley) have gone to talk to pirate radio stations and people who believe in black helicopters coming to get them (I'm watching you, Steve) in an attempt to whip up these angry, marginal but highly energetic voters. These people have energy and enthusiasm, but have no idea how to use those things productively. So we end up with LePage supporters engaging in activity like berating high-profile state lawmakers and trashing grade schools. This is one of the reasons that I am deathly afraid of Paul LePage winning the primary."

But even as reporters and LePage's new general election political opponents began to focus on his questionable conduct and associations, there emerged new dynamics that mitigated the damage they might cause.

The first of these was that almost the entire Republican establishment, including all of LePage's primary opponents, quickly got behind his candidacy. A week after the primary, all six defeated candidates gathered with LePage on the steps of the Waterville City Hall for a unity press conference and gave unequivocal endorsements of his campaign. Despite the fact that there would eventually be three independent candidates in the race, some claiming conservative credentials, very few moderate Republicans jumped ship. (A notable exception would be former party chair Mark Ellis, who endorsed independent Shawn Moody.) LePage's new Tea Party supporters weren't going anywhere, and if he could marry them to the traditionally more moderate wing of his party, he would have a powerful electoral coalition going into the general election.

The full-throated support of his party and of national groups like the Republican Governors Association (RGA) made up for the leanness of his campaign. The GOP brought in experienced voices that helped to professionalize his mostly-volunteer electoral operation. The RGA set up a political action committee (PAC) that allowed out-of-state corporations to make large contributions and engaged in third-party spending to reinforce LePage's relatively small campaign war chest.

Contributions to the PAC, totaling $1.8 million, included large outlays from the pharmaceutical industry and from companies profiting from the privatization of government services, including $19,000 from for-profit virtual school management company K12 Education. Their interests would be well represented in the LePage administration.

Other contributions came from companies and groups (including the Michigan Chamber of Commerce) with no obvious or direct interest in Maine state policy but with ties to national conservative organizations, including the American Legislative Exchange Council (ALEC) and the U.S. Chamber of Commerce.

Both of Maine's moderate Republican senators, Olympia Snowe and Susan Collins, would also publicly endorse LePage, raise money for his campaign, and appear with him at public events.

The second new advantage for LePage's campaign came with the Democrats' nomination of Senator Elizabeth "Libby" Mitchell. Mitchell had come out on top in a five-way Democratic primary, winning nearly as many votes and almost as large a percentage of her primary electorate as LePage had of his. While the Republican had campaigned as an agent of change and had energized new voters, however, Mitchell won based on the strength of a long and distinguished career in politics.

The seventy-year-old Mitchell had first been elected to the Maine State House of Representatives in 1974 and had twice run unsuccessfully for federal office–for the U.S. Senate in 1984 and for Congress in 1990. In 1996 she had been the first woman to become speaker of the Maine house, and in 2008 she was elected president of the state senate, making her the first woman in any state in the country to have held both positions.

Distinguished service of that caliber would ordinarily be a political asset, but in the 2010 election, with a national anti-incumbent mood, an unpopular outgoing Democratic governor, and four opponents who had never held state elected office, her public service became a target for attack. She was a perfect foil, in particular, for the Tea Party–fueled message of throw-out-the-bums change that LePage embodied.

And Mitchell had another, bigger problem to cope with.

Maine voters have a history, unique in the country, of voting in significant numbers for independent candidates for elected office. In 1974 they elected independent James B. Longley as governor. In 1992 Ross Perot came in second in the presidential contest in the state, winning his highest percentage of the vote anywhere in the country and placing ahead of sitting President George H.W. Bush. In 1994 and again in 1998, Mainers elected independent Angus King as governor. (In 2012 King reentered the political arena, winning the U.S. Senate race to replace retiring Senator Olympia Snowe with 53 percent of the vote.) Most statewide races in the last decade have included at least one independent or third-party candidate.

Three independent candidates entered the 2010 race. By far the most formidable was Eliot Cutler, a millionaire corporate lawyer who had grown up in Maine but had spent most of his life in Washington, D.C., first working for Maine Senator Edmund Muskie and President Jimmy Carter and then founding his own law practice, which he eventually merged with legal and lobbying powerhouse Akin Gump. Cutler became a partner in the global firm and spent three years living in Beijing and overseeing Akin Gump's interests in China. His message during the campaign was simple: a pox on both your houses. According to Cutler, party politics had broken government, and he had both the experience and new ideas necessary to fix it.

In addition to his national political and corporate connections and his personal fortune, Cutler also had the advantage of close ties with the owners of the *Bangor Daily News* and with Maine Today Media, owners of the *Portland Press Herald, Waterville Morning Sentinel,* and *Kennebec Journal.* The Bangor and Portland publications are the state's two largest daily newspapers.

The Maine Today papers in particular, led by CEO Richard Connor, seemed determined to boost Cutler's campaign. In addition to multiple pro-Cutler opinion pieces penned by Connor himself, the papers' news divisions covered Cutler's campaign more often and with a friendlier tone than his opponents. At one point a *Press Herald* reporter even asked that his name be removed from a pro-Cutler story that the paper's editors had insisted go to press with statements from anonymous sources. The article ran without a byline.

Colorful and caustic Maine media critic Al Diamon accused Connor of engaging in "outrageous grandstanding for Eliot Cutler's gubernatorial campaign, allowing his bias to leak from the editorial page to the news section." Diamon declared it to be the most significant example of blatant bias in Maine's media in recent memory.

Cutler is socially liberal, hails from southern Maine, and is a former Democrat (although he also briefly registered as a Republican), and so in 2010 he was much more likely to contest for votes with Mitchell than with LePage (although he also argued during his campaign for smaller government and lower taxes).

And contest he did. Although he trailed the two major-party candidates in public polls for most of the race, Cutler experienced a sharp rise in support in the last few weeks before the election as he aired television ads and gained newspaper endorsements. Mitchell's support decreased at a similar rate.

LePage's support, meanwhile, remained relatively stable throughout the campaign, though there was a dip in late September and early October after he made a series of controversial comments. In separate incidents, he swore at one public radio reporter, said he was "about ready to punch" another, and declared that, if elected, he would tell President Obama to "go to hell."

The LePage campaign mitigated these public and media eruptions at the end of the campaign through the simple expedient of severely limiting the candidate's exposure to the public and the media. He declined to sit for newspaper endorsement interviews and cancelled his debate appearances, including the only live statewide television debate on the Maine Public Broadcasting Network. It worked. The less people heard from LePage, the more his numbers recovered.

In the last week of the campaign, the polling trends for LePage's two main opponents intensified. Cutler's numbers shot up quickly as Mitchell's fell. A number of factors were at play, but three nearly simultaneous events in the last week stand out as significant reasons for the shift.

The first was a series of Democratic Party attack mailers that criticized Cutler's firm for its lobbying on behalf of Chinese companies and its work to export jobs. The language and imagery in the mailers, including photos of fortune cookies and fake Chinese script, was xenophobic, bordering on racist. They played right into Cutler's arguments about what was wrong with partisan politics, and they offered tangible proof that the Democratic Party considered him a serious candidate and a real electoral threat.

Mitchell, who ran using public financing under Maine's Clean Elections Act, had little control over what her party did on her behalf. The Mitchell campaign had focused on an electability argument against Cutler, contending that moderates and progressives had to come together to defeat LePage and that a vote for Cutler was really a vote for the Tea Party. As Mitchell failed to overcome LePage's lead and as Cutler's campaign continued to benefit from good press and improving poll numbers, her rationale was turned on its head.

This controversy contributed to the second ground-shifting event. Saying that the mail attacks had pushed him over the edge, on the Saturday before the election former independent governor Angus King announced that he was endorsing Cutler and would join him on the campaign trail for the last few days of the election. King, one of the most popular figures in Maine politics, made the case for Cutler's independence and electability better than anyone else possibly could.

The third event was an e-mail sent to the list of the largest LGBT (lesbian, gay, bisexual, and transgender) rights organization in the state, Equality Maine, on the day before the election. The organization, which had built a massive statewide following the year before during an unsuccessful same-sex marriage referendum, had previously endorsed Mitchell. Now, however, Equality Maine announced that the most important consideration was to beat LePage and prevent him from rolling back protections for LGBT Mainers. The organization noted that Cutler also supported gay rights and marriage equality and that he was ahead in the latest polls. It was a clear signal to progressive voters that Cutler was the strategic choice. For many it was the last word they heard as they headed into the voting booths.

If the election had been held even a few days later, the outcome might have been different, but in the end even Cutler's meteoric rise wasn't fast enough. Although he performed almost a full ten points better than he had in polls taken just a few days before, he fell just short of LePage's total.

LePage won with 38 percent of the vote, Cutler came in second with 36 percent, Mitchell garnered 19 percent, and the two other independent candidates, Shawn Moody and Kevin Scott, won 5 percent and 1 percent respectively. It was a long election night, and Cutler led early as more populous southern areas reported their returns first. LePage's total, however, ticked up throughout the night as more rural towns reported, and the next day he was declared the seventy-fourth governor of the state of Maine.

LePage's strategy of continuing to play to his base with hard-line conservative policies and divisive public statements couldn't have succeeded without the other candidates splitting the vote, but they did, and it did.

chapter 5
Transition and Influences

T he transition from campaigning to governing went relatively smoothly for LePage, especially considering that it had been sixteen years since a Republican had held the office. The change proved difficult, however, for many of his Tea Party supporters.

One of the reasons for this was that LePage relied heavily on a group of establishment figures to manage the transition process and then take on the key roles in his new administration. The three co-chairs of his transition team were John Butera, a close associate who headed the Central Maine Growth Council; Ann Robinson, a lawyer and lobbyist with the firm Preti Flaherty; and Tarren Bragdon, CEO of the Maine Heritage Policy Center (MHPC), a conservative interest group. Although MHPC is known for their hard-right policies and had participated in a number of Tea Party events, they were viewed as too mainstream by many in the Tea Party movement. Both Robinson and Bragdon have close ties to national corporate, conservative political networks, including the American Legislative Exchange Council, the corporate-backed conservative organization dedicated to influencing state-level policy.

Tea Party figures were mostly relegated to ceremonial roles in the transition. Those with real power in the fledgling administration were more often mainstream Republicans or those who had been part of LePage's circle in Waterville before he had begun to court Tea Party support.

"Paul was listening to the Republicans that had been around a long time," said Carter Jones. "He obviously wanted the Republican support, and Paul was probably thinking he should buddy up to them more than the guys like me who were trying to change the direction. The reason why we won is we weren't the establishment. We were the people who were trying to redirect the government."

LePage may not have had much of a choice. Most of his hardcore Tea Party supporters lacked the background and expertise needed to make sure his new administration got off the ground, and they would also have brought additional volatility to an administration that already had plenty. Tea Party leader Pete Harring was named to the transition advisory committee but was not hired for a post in the administration, perhaps because of a series of offensive and occasionally violent online comments Harring had made about liberals, Senator Snowe, and President Obama that came to light during the transition period.

"I think that was window dressing and that was bullshit," said Cynthia Rosen of Harring's role in the transition. "After that transition team, your normal Joe just faded out of the picture."

Not all of the Tea Partiers faded out of the LePage administration. One of them went out with a bang.

Philip Congdon was one of the very few Tea Party stalwarts to last beyond the transition. He was appointed by LePage to be commissioner of Maine's Department of Economic and Community Development, an important post for an administration that had promised to be business-friendly and increase economic opportunity.

Congdon's appointment was based on his Tea Party ties and personal relationship with the governor and was made despite his complete lack of experience in the economic development portfolio. LePage had met the retired Texas Instruments engineer at a Waldoboro meeting of the Maine Constitutionalists, a Tea Party group focused on encouraging strict adherence to their interpretation of America's founding documents in order to defeat what they termed a "socialist agenda."

This political familiarity with LePage seemed to be Congdon's main qualification for the post, as he lacked even basic experience with several important aspects of the job to which he was appointed.

"As far as community economic development, I'll tell you right now, I haven't done it. But I'll also tell you that I am convinced that I can," Congdon said at his confirmation hearings. He also revealed that while he had experience with large companies and managing personnel, he had no familiarity with small businesses or the tourism industry, two of Maine's major economic engines.

"I haven't thought about it," Congdon replied when asked how he would attract businesses to rural Maine, including far-northern Aroostook County.

Asked about his ties to the radical Constitutionalist group, Congdon said he had stopped attending meetings after the organization was "taken over" by the John Birch Society.

"I don't own a tinfoil hat," he assured the committee.

Nine senators in the 35-member body, all Democrats, voted against Congdon's nomination, but his appointment was ratified by the Republican majority.

Soon after he became commissioner, Congdon apparently did a great deal more thinking about rural economic development. Unfortunately, he then chose to share his thoughts in public, torpedoing his tenure as commissioner and proving just how dangerous it can be to appoint to such a vital post someone whose only political experience is through the Tea Party.

In a swing through northern Maine in early April, Congdon attended a Chamber of Commerce gathering in Caribou and met with officials at Northern Maine Community College. He made a series of off-color remarks at the two events, including offensive statements about rural Mainers and black people.

"The problem with higher education today dates back to the civil rights movement in the '60s that allowed blacks to enter colleges. That resulted in the large amount of remedial education required in colleges," said Congdon, according to a letter sent to LePage by Representative John Martin, an Aroostook County Democrat who was made aware of Congdon's remarks.

"People in Aroostook County ought to get the hell off the reservation and create jobs for Aroostook County. You have not done a good job of educating your kids," was another quote from Congdon. This was taken as a slight against rural Mainers in general and the state's Native American population in particular.

After LePage received Martin's letter, Congdon was asked for his resignation. His dismissal was announced in the ninth paragraph of a press release from the governor's office, and LePage refused to discuss the issue further.

"We had a personnel issue, we dealt with it. Let's move on," is all he would say when questioned by reporters.

Congdon was one of a trio of commissioners appointed at the beginning of LePage's term who were forced to resign within a matter of months. The others were Department of Environmental Protection Commissioner Darryl Brown and Department of Marine Resources Commissioner Norman Olsen. Each story is interesting in its own right, and each helps illuminate the mix of competing influences that has governed the LePage administration.

It's difficult to boil down any politician or administration into a set of inputs and outputs, especially when the actor is as impulsive as LePage. Three things that seem to have significant effects on his administration's decisions, however, include the ideology and anger of his core supporters in the Tea Party; the influence of corporate interests and their representatives within his administration; and LePage's personal style, including his aggressive persistence and black-and-white worldview.

Brown's resignation as DEP commissioner was the least controversial of the three and came because of his business interests. As a development consultant with clients who had recently applied for permits under the federal Clean Water Act, he was found to be violating state conflict-of-interest law and was ineligible to hold the office to which he had been appointed. LePage subsequently made Brown head of the State Planning Office and appointed lobbyist Patricia Aho (someone with even more of a substantive conflict of interest, although not one prohibited by law) to replace him at the DEP.

Olsen's problem was his attitude. He shared much of LePage's hard-charging aggression but lacked even a scrap of the everyman authenticity that made the governor an effective grassroots politician. Olsen's crime was angering Maine's lobstermen, a powerful constituency, by making definitive public statements in favor of allowing the landing of lobster bycatch by fishing trawlers (a policy he and LePage agree on but Maine lobstermen oppose) and refusing to negotiate the issue or hear their complaints.

Angered by Olsen's policies and attitude, more than a hundred fishermen signed a letter of concern to Governor LePage. Olsen says he was then cut off within the administration. LePage took constituency meetings without him and refused to include him on policy discussions. Finally, in July of LePage's first year in office, Olsen resigned. He penned a 1,600-word parting shot at the governor, accusing him of abandoning his policy priorities, succumbing to interest group pressure, and maintaining a personal vendetta against the city of Portland (where the bycatch would be landed) because of the politics of the liberal-leaning city. LePage denied most of these charges.

One commissioner resigned because of his close corporate ties. Another, a Tea Party activist, found himself out of his depth in state government. The third was outspoken and combative and didn't seem to know when to keep his mouth shut. In a way, each of these early retirements can be seen as representing some of the most troubling aspects of LePage's style of governance and the administration he has built.

While LePage's combativeness, similar to Olsen's, and his controversial public statements, similar to Congdon's, have garnered the most media attention, it is perhaps Brown's example that relates most directly to the conduct of his administration.

LePage isn't shy about his corporate deference, calling it "cutting red tape" or being "open for business." The result is an administration deeply influenced by corporate lobbyists, many playing a role directly in government, as well as national corporate groups like the American Legislative Exchange Council. While this may seem at odds with LePage's grassroots, Tea Party pedigree, it's actually one more way in which his career has mirrored the national movement. LePage's administration, much like the national Tea Party, has been influenced by and in many ways subsumed in the interests of the corporations and wealthy donors that provide both funding and the ideological infrastructure on which they have both relied.

These corporate influences were noticeable from the first days of LePage's transition into office and can be clearly seen in many of his policies, particularly his attempts to roll back environmental protections, divert education funding to for-profit schools, break Maine's labor unions, and deregulate health insurance.

chapter 6 Transparency

Paul LePage ran on a platform of transparency in government. "Every Maine citizen has a right to know what government is up to," read his campaign website. "He will fight for stronger laws to protect and expand Maine citizens' right to access information from state and local government. When Paul is Governor, open government will be a reality, not a talking point."

Shortly after he won the general election, LePage reiterated those guarantees and announced that he was launching the most transparent administration in Maine history.

He got off on the right foot. Unlike previous Maine governors, LePage placed a limit of $9,500 on individual contributions given to his transition organization and disclosed the names of people and businesses that gave to the fund (although not the amounts they gave). The state of Maine provides a governor-elect with only $5,000 to cover transition expenses, and incoming administrations have often relied on private fundraising to make up the rest of the cost of staff and offices.

Thanks to LePage's disclosures, for the first time Mainers had a glimpse of who was paying to fund a governor's transition to power. For the most part, it was exactly who might be expected: corporations and lobby organizations with interests in Augusta–everyone from BP and AT&T to L.L. Bean and the Maine Pulp and Paper Association.

In comparison with campaign contributions, donations to a transition fund are less obviously an expression of the donor individual or company's political beliefs. After all, the election has already been won. The payment goes directly to staff and expenses, is solicited just as a new administration is developing its policy priorities, and could certainly be seen as an attempt to influence government.

It could be argued that the businesses that contributed simply care about good governance and funded the transition out of a sense of civic responsibility, without any hope of reciprocation. But this would be an optimistic interpretation for most of the businesses that contributed, and for some it's outright laughable. Florida-based plastic pallet maker iGPS, for instance, gave to the transition fund and has no obvious presence or interest in Maine except for its attempts to stymie implementation of the state's Kid-Safe Products Act regulating the use of dangerous chemicals in consumer products.

Another contributor, listed as "Mallinckrodt," appears to be Mallinckrodt LLC. At the time of the contribution, it was a subsidiary of multinational medical device manufacturer Covidien and a corporate entity that manufactured no products and had no regular employees in Maine. Its main purpose seemed to be fighting the state-mandated cleanup of mercury pollution at the site of the former HoltraChem chemical plant—previously owned by Mallinckrodt—on the banks of the Penobscot River in Orrington.

Another out-of-state contributor with few ties to Maine at the time was LogistiCare Solutions, LLC, a medical transportation company. LogistiCare was later awarded a $5.1 million contract by the LePage administration to provide nonemergency transportation to Medicaid patients, a service previously provided through contracts with local nonprofits. The decision to privatize the service proved disastrous, as LogistiCare and fellow private rides broker Coordinated Transportation Solutions (CTS) badly mismanaged their contracts, prompting thousands of complaints and leaving sick Mainers stranded and waiting for rides that never came.

For the first time, thanks to the LePage administration's disclosure, Maine people were able to see these contributions, learn who was funding their governor's incoming transition, and understand what the donors might be asking for in return.

The transition transparency didn't last long, however. In March 2011, an amendment to the corporate records of LePage Transition 2010 was filed. The nonprofit corporation was renamed Maine People Before Politics (a reference to one of LePage's slogans from his campaign) and in its new incarnation became the governor's personal interest group. LePage's chief strategist, Brent Littlefield, oversaw the group, and former Marden's employee and LePage campaign staffer Jason Savage managed day-to-day operations (until 2013, when he left to become executive director of the Maine Republican Party). Rather than just paying for staff and office space during the transition, the leftover money from corporate donors could now be used for the direct political support of Governor LePage and his policies, and new money could be given anonymously to the same accounts that LePage had once promised to make public.

Maine People Before Politics (MPBP) has acted as LePage's shadow campaign ever since, running television ads lauding the governor, pressuring state legislators to vote his way on key pieces of legislation, and attempting to maintain some of the grassroots involvement and momentum from the 2010 campaign, although not to the degree many of his Tea Party supporters had wanted.

Littlefield continued to serve as a strategic advisor to MPBP even as he took on the same role for LePage's official reelection campaign. The dark money group allowed LePage's individual and corporate supporters to give money anonymously and to do so at times and in amounts that would be prohibited by campaign finance laws if the money were given directly to his campaign.

LePage's shift away from transparency was also obvious in his response to some of the first Freedom of Access submissions to his new administration. Requests by journalists and the Conservation Law Foundation to view documents related to the administration's formulation of environmental policies were stymied by LePage's insistence that he wouldn't turn over documents from the transition period, even though they had been in the possession of state employees since his inauguration. When the documents were eventually released, they painted an unflattering picture of the power of lobbyists and corporate interests in driving the administration's legislative and regulatory priorities. (See Chapter 7.)

In 2013, LePage completely and finally turned his back on the principles espoused in his initial call for transparency, vetoing two bills that would have required the disclosure of donations to future gubernatorial transitions. In his veto message for one of these bills, LePage said that instituting such a requirement would be an affront to the integrity of new governors and would disrespect the voting public.

"When Maine voters speak at the ballot box, their newly elected officials should be trusted to do the right thing," wrote LePage.

The other bill, initially passed without opposition in the Maine House and Senate, would have increased the penalties for candidates and PACs that miss deadlines for reporting expenditures close to an election. This proposed legislation was meant to discourage the late reporting of large political expenditures, such as in 2010 when the Republican State Leadership Committee made a last-minute expenditure of $160,000 in five key Maine senate races, failed to report their spending on time, and faced only a small fine.

In his veto message, LePage said that he opposed strengthening the regulations because people might make unsupported claims about ethics violations in order to tarnish political opponents, a nonsensical argument that the *Bangor Daily News* likened to "blaming the referee, who's trying to ensure that a game is being played fairly, for the actions of players who commit fouls."

LePage did take some other steps to improve transparency and accountability. In 2011 he worked with Democratic House Minority Leader Emily Cain to pass a new ethics bill, increasing the financial reporting requirements for legislators and executive branch officials.

In 2013, his administration launched the Maine Open Checkbook website, providing information on payments to government personnel and vendors. The site isn't user-friendly in its current iteration, and searches are as likely to end with an error message as with useful information, but it's a step toward making state government data available online. It has the potential to grow into an important resource.

But these steps represent far less than the new paradigm of transparency that LePage promised, and, on the whole, the policies, practices, and statements of the governor and his administration have taken the state backward on the public and media's ability to access information about state government.

For example, LePage makes a point of communicating without using state e-mail and usually doesn't take notes at meetings so that fewer documents are available for the public to access through Maine's Freedom of Access law. He also gives few interviews and has repeatedly threatened to cut off access to media outlets whose coverage he doesn't like.

LePage's refusal to meet early in 2012 with the incoming Democratic speaker of the house and senate president was in part because the Democratic Party had begun sending a staff member to record his statements at public events.

LePage's position on transparency has also been made clear by his repeated verbal and political attacks on Maine's Freedom of Access Act (FOAA). In March 2011, at a statutory meeting with the heads of Maine's legislative and judicial branches, LePage complained about the number and content of reporters' FOAA requests and, according to some of those present at the meeting, surprised other attendees by declaring that "FOAA is being used as a form of internal terrorism."

Also that month, LePage created a controversy when he attempted to exempt his Business Advisory Council from FOAA by executive order. The new advisory board, made up of twenty-one representatives of corporate interests chosen by the governor, was slated to meet regularly with the commissioners of the Department of Economic and Community Development and the Department of Labor in order to inform the administration's policy agenda. Media outlets and transparency advocates immediately objected, and the Maine Today newspapers argued in a letter to the governor that the exemptions "violate both the letter and the spirit of Maine's Freedom of Access Act, and also violate the state and federal constitutional rights of Maine's citizens." LePage eventually backed down and shelved his plans for the advisory group.

In 2012, LePage submitted a bill to the legislature that would have kept his working papers, memos, and other governor's office documents hidden, in some cases until the end of the legislative session. It was eventually rejected by a wide margin in the Republican-controlled house of representatives. One Republican lawmaker, speaking on the floor of the house, called it "a bill only Richard Nixon would allow."

In 2013, the LePage administration gave a $925,000 no-bid contract to a conservative operative to evaluate Maine's health care and public assistance programs, starting with a report on Maine's Medicaid program. LePage's staff received the final version of the report in December but refused to release it or previous drafts for weeks, despite repeated Freedom of Access requests from reporters. The staff gave no statutory reason for the delay, prompting Maine Attorney General Janet Mills to announce that the administration was violating the law by continuing to refuse the requests.

"As chief law enforcement officer for the State of Maine and chief advisor on Freedom of Access issues, I must insist you release this report to all who request it immediately," wrote Mills.

"Tell her to sue me," was LePage's response to Mills's warning. He delivered that message at a press conference to which reporters who had been requesting the documents were not invited.

While LePage has taken some steps toward increased transparency, any broad evaluation of his administration shows that public access to information about Maine's government has been reduced, and only public and media pressure and legislative action have stopped him from reducing it further. Rather than fulfilling his promise of running the most transparent administration in history, his governorship has been among the most opaque. In 2013, national watchdog group Citizens for Responsibility and Ethics in Washington (CREW) released a report on government ethics rating LePage as the second-worst governor in the country, in large part because of his disdain for transparency.

chapter 7 The Environment

At the Kennebec County Republican Party Caucus in March 2010, gubernatorial candidate Paul LePage told a horrifying story of anti-business government overreach by Maine's Department of Environmental Protection.

"In 1992, I was running a power plant in Eastern Maine, the DEP comes up and says you know we'd like you to do a study," said LePage, speaking about one of his consulting jobs. "So it cost us fifty more thousand dollars and June, July, and August to count all the buffaloes in Maine. Lo and behold we found one, at the Acadia Zoo in Trenton. The next spring they come up and say now that you've been so successful with the buffalo, we'd like you to count black flies."

It was a well-practiced performance (this being far from the first time LePage had shared his buffalo study anecdote), and his delivery was pitch-perfect. He painted a compelling picture of his reaction as a plainspoken, no-nonsense businessman confronted with absurd requests from government officials who knew nothing of the real world. Details such as managing to find a single buffalo (and, in some versions of the story, identifying sixteen species of black flies) gave the story an aura of verisimilitude and made it likely to stick with those who heard it. The story perfectly made LePage's case that government and environmentalists had gone too far and that a radical restructuring of environmental regulations was needed.

The only problem with the story, as with many of LePage's anecdotes, is that it never happened.

A few months later, LePage told the same story to Maine Public Radio reporter Susan Sharon as an example of a company put out of business by the excessive regulations of the Maine DEP. When Sharon dug into the details, however, she found that almost everything the governor said was wrong. The DEP had ordered no such studies, or any study of buffaloes and black flies, ever. When she spoke to the former owner of the peat-fired power plant LePage was referring to, she found they didn't go out of business because of government regulations but because of logistical problems with harvesting enough peat.

The buffalo study story, like many of LePage's false anecdotes, offered little in the way of real-world policy prescriptions. There weren't actually any mandatory buffalo studies, so what change was he really proposing?

As a candidate, LePage stuck mostly to speaking in general terms about making government more business-friendly and getting rid of unspecified harmful regulations. Once he became governor, however, LePage addressed this lack of specificity by outsourcing the work of selecting which environmental regulations should be targeted to a group of people who had plenty of ideas: corporate lobbyists.

Ann Robinson is the chair of the Government Affairs Practice Group at Maine's largest lobbying firm, Preti Flaherty. She's also a member of the board of directors of the Maine Chamber of Commerce and has been active at a high level in the Maine GOP for decades, including serving as the party's lawyer, as chair of their 2008 convention, and as the GOP nominee for attorney general in 1996.

Robinson was exactly the kind of establishment figure LePage needed to help him make the transition from running one of the more informal and distributed campaigns that Maine had seen in recent memory to operating the levers of power in state government.

It's not listed on her official biography, but according to documents obtained and published by the Center for Media and Democracy, Robinson also began serving as Maine co-chair of the American Legislative Exchange Council (ALEC) in the summer of 2011. ALEC is a national organization made up of corporate lobbyists and conservative politicians funded in part by conservative megadonors Charles and David Koch. It serves as a conduit for corporate-backed legislation to be pumped into state legislatures. The secretive group receives funding from a host of corporate interests, including oil, tobacco, telecom, and drug companies, as well as from conservative interest groups such as the National Rifle Association and the Family Research Council.

Robinson and her firm represented many of these same corporate interests on environmental and other issues in Maine. For example, she served as a lobbyist for the Pharmaceutical Research and Manufacturers of America (PhRMA), Merck, and the Toy Industry Association of America in their fight against the passage of Maine's Kid-Safe Products Act, a law that regulates the use of dangerous chemicals in everyday products.

As other members of LePage's transition team, including Maine Heritage Policy Center director Tarren Bragdon and lobbyist Kathleen Newman (who would later become the administration's legislative director), began planning LePage's first budget, Robinson took over the crafting of LePage's regulatory agenda.

According to reporting by Colin Woodard in the *Portland Phoenix* newspaper, based on transition documents obtained through a Freedom of Access request, Robinson assembled a subcommittee within the transition to focus on eliminating environmental regulations. It was chaired by fellow lobbyist Gloria Pinza. Pinza's firm, Pierce Atwood, lobbied for a number of similarly interested clients including the American Petroleum Institute and the American Chemistry Council.

The governor and his daughter and deputy chief of staff, Lauren LePage, submitted a memo to Robinson on the kind of legislation they wanted to see, but it was more an ideological framework with few specific recommendations. Little of their language made it into the final bill.

Instead, the majority of the regulatory proposals that were eventually announced by the LePage administration were written word-for-word by Preti Flaherti and Pierce Atwood lobbyists. The final product would include a broad attempt to roll back all Maine environmental laws and regulations to match weaker federal standards, a new statute of limitations on lawsuits on environmental violations, and a provision to eliminate the Board of Environmental Protection, a body meant to provide citizen oversight of DEP actions and decisions on environmental issues. It also included a number of proposals written by lobbyists to implement more specific goals of the corporations they represented.

LePage's controversial proposal to require that no less than thirty percent of the land overseen by Maine's Land Use Regulatory Commission (the agency charged with balancing economic development and environmental protection in Maine's North Woods) be rezoned for development, for instance, was apparently submitted on behalf of two companies with significant land holdings in northern Maine: H.C. Haynes and W.T. Gardner & Sons.

The Kid-Safe Products Act, a target for a number of national chemical and manufacturing concerns with powerful lobbyists, was another high-profile law slated for repeal, as was a new rule arising from its regulatory framework that would ban the use of Bisphenol-A (BPA), an endocrine-disrupting chemical, in children's products.

When the initial package of regulatory rollbacks was announced (it was dubbed "Phase One" by the LePage administration), Maine environmentalists and legislative observers were stunned by the scope of the proposals. Virtually no aspect of the state's environmental and conservation regulations had gone untouched. If implemented, the proposals would nullify decades of hard-won environmental protections and standards.

Although the likely effects of the proposals were obvious, no one outside the LePage administration would have known the genesis of the effort if not for a mistake on Robinson's part. She compiled the proposals on the computer at her office at Preti Flaherty, and her software included a small numeric code, meant for billing purposes, in the bottom-left corner of one version of the document that was distributed to legislators. A sharp-eyed Democratic representative realized what the code was and figured out where the document must have originated.

Luckily, the Republican-controlled legislature was not as willing to let lobbyists do their jobs for them as was LePage. Public outrage over the proposals led to a watering-down of most of them. The version of the plan that was eventually introduced as Legislative Document 1 that session was missing some of the most controversial proposals, and the bills that were eventually passed were even more moderate.

Some significant deregulation bills did make it into law, however, including a new five-year statute of limitations on environmental violations that would make it easier for corporate polluters to avoid legal responsibility for their actions. Maine's pesticide notification registry was repealed, and the two public seats were removed from the Board of Pesticide Control. A bill that would eventually lead to the weakening of Maine's Land Use Regulatory Commission was also passed, although it was far more modest than what LePage had originally proposed.

In other areas, LePage's rollbacks made little headway. The new rule restricting BPA in children's products was passed by a wide majority in the legislature, and the Kid-Safe Products Act, rather than being repealed, was actually strengthened. This result was likely due in large part to a verbal misstep by LePage.

"There's not been any science that identifies that there's a problem," said LePage at a press conference in February 2011. "The only thing that I've heard is if you take a plastic bottle, put it in the microwave and then heat it up it gives off a chemical similar to estrogen, and so I mean worst case is some women might have little beards."

LePage couldn't have designed a better soundbite to highlight both the dangers of the toxic chemical and his flippant attitude toward its regulation. The "little beards" remark, as it came to be known, made national news and prompted a public backlash that included a memorable online campaign in which thousands of Maine women posted photos of themselves wearing fake beards.

Other provocative actions by LePage included firing the medical director of MaineCare, who had previously testified in favor of the BPA ban, and removing information on the dangers of BPA from a state website. These actions prompted additional negative attention to his policies on toxic chemicals. In the end he was forced to use his veto to stop the Republican-controlled legislature from moving in the opposite direction and strengthening the Kid-Safe Products Act. Republicans in the Maine Senate subsequently upheld his veto and scuttled the reinforced law.

While less than completely successful, "Phase One," as the name implied, was just the beginning of LePage's move to degrade Maine's environmental protections. It was also just the beginning of lobbyist influence on his environmental priorities.

Woodard's investigations into the influence of lobbyists on LePage administration environmental policies were also just beginning, and in June 2013 he released a new series of articles on the continued pervasive influence of corporate interests within the administration. Among the revelations contained in the series, which was published in the *Portland Press Herald,* was that Department of Environmental Protection Commissioner Patricia Aho, a former lobbyist at Pierce Atwood, had repeatedly used the bureaucracy she controlled to advance corporate interests.

According to the reporting, Aho implemented what can only be described as a reign of terror to get the department's expert staff in line with her and LePage's new priorities. One employee quoted in the *Press Herald* compared it to the Khmer Rouge. Staff were verbally humiliated by new political appointees, reassigned from their areas of expertise, and pressured not to enforce certain environmental regulations or give testimony before the state legislature. Under Aho, political appointees, rather than technical staff, were put in charge of making environmental policy recommendations. Within six months of LePage assuming office, 85 of the department's approximately 400 employees were no longer working for the DEP.

Many of the regulatory and enforcement areas that saw the biggest changes were those in which Aho's former clients had the greatest interest. For example, during her lobbying career she had worked for the American Chemistry Council, AstraZeneca Pharmaceuticals, the American Petroleum Institute, and lead paint manufacturer Millennium Holdings to oppose the Kid-Safe Products Act. Once she was appointed to the DEP, Aho did everything possible to frustrate the popular law.

One of the most blatant actions taken by the new administration was, after their attempts to dismantle it legislatively had failed, to refuse to recommend new chemicals for regulation under the act. Aho claimed the department didn't have the resources to implement this portion of the law, but one class of toxins, brominated flame retardants (which are known to have carcinogenic and endocrine disrupting effects), had already been thoroughly investigated and slated for regulatory enforcement by DEP staff before LePage took office. Rather than allow the new regulations to go forward, LePage and Aho spiked the department's previous findings and recommendations and allowed use of the chemicals to continue without oversight.

In 2013, when the DEP finally did recommended four new substances to be named as "priority chemicals" under the law, the exercise amounted to little more than a smokescreen. The toxins targeted, including mercury, arsenic, cadmium, and formaldehyde, were already mostly regulated or banned by the federal government and had virtually no presence in children's products, allowing Aho and LePage to claim they were obeying the letter of the law without actually taking any new steps to protect children's health or inconvenience Aho's former clients.

Eventually LePage's DEP would drop even its plans to regulate the carcinogen formaldehyde after lobbying by chemical firms, including Koch Industries, the industrial conglomerate owned by David and Charles Koch.

Another troubling action taken by Aho to frustrate toxins regulation was revealed in a lawsuit filed by Andrea Lani, a DEP employee who was in charge of implementing the Kid-Safe Products Act when LePage took office. In 2011, Lani used vacation time to testify before the legislature against the administration's attempt to dismantle the act, a right of all government employees protected by state law. After her testimony before the committee, Lani was removed from her position in the department and reassigned to a clerical job handling public records requests. She was replaced with a less-qualified employee, and a political appointee was given oversight over the toxins file. Any real progress on strengthening the regulations quickly ground to a halt. In 2012, the state settled the lawsuit over Lani's demotion, paying her $65,000 in noneconomic damages.

Another example of the DEP advancing the interests of Aho's corporate clients, also unearthed by Woodard's investigation, was the department's failure to make submissions to the federal government before key dam relicensing deadlines. Regulation of dams is managed at the federal level, but once every quarter century the state is given an opportunity to intervene and request authority to manage water levels in reservoirs and rivers. In at least three instances after LePage took office, the Maine DEP failed to file submissions in time and missed the window, waiving the state's rights for a generation.

The failure to meet the submission deadline for a dam on Flagstaff Lake was particularly galling. Florida Power & Light, owners of the Long Falls Dam, had been allowing the lake to drain to levels that rendered it unfit for recreational use by residents of the lakefront town of Eustis, replacing the former shorelines with foul-smelling mudflats. Locals had fought the company's practices for a decade and seemed on the verge of winning, despite the company having hired the heavy-hitters at Pierce Atwood to represent them, but that was before Aho moved into the DEP.

In November 2011, the department missed the federal deadline and gave up Maine's rights to manage the water levels at Flagstaff Lake. Aho would later argue that it was a simple clerical oversight, but records obtained by the *Press Herald* showed that there was plenty of advance notice. Aho had been briefed on the matter by her staff, and the DEP had even received a last-minute warning from the attorney general's office that they were about to miss the deadline. The records also revealed that Aho had met personally with a former Pierce Atwood colleague who represented FP&L to discuss the issue.

Aho, Robinson, and other lobbyists didn't always have a monopoly on control over administration environmental policies. On some issues, decisions seemed to be driven less by corporate interests and more by LePage's Tea Party ideology. This influence is particularly clear on the issue of commercial wind power.

Thanks to local geography, corporate investment, and government encouragement, Maine stood poised in 2010 to become a leader in wind power development and technology. A U.S. Department of Energy report released that year found Maine to have the highest potential power generation by wind of any state in New England, and a new state wind development plan and renewable energy standards had led to wind turbines sprouting in clusters throughout the state.

The new development, however, led to a backlash from residents of rural areas near existing and proposed wind power sites. They saw the turbines as government-subsidized eyesores encroaching on their neighborhoods and scenery. These complaints happened to fit well with the antigovernment views and rural constituency of the Tea Party and were bolstered by the belief, prevalent on the far right, that manmade global climate change was either overblown or a complete myth pushed by the liberal elites in order to erode personal liberties. The anti-wind and Tea Party groups amplified each other's messages, and as LePage ran for governor, they coalesced to form a small but vocal single-issue political constituency.

LePage sought to appeal to these interests from the beginning of his campaign. He railed against wind power and declared in a radio interview that "I don't know if global warming is a myth or not, but I will say this: I do not believe in the Al Gore science."

Once in office, LePage stuck with his anti-science agenda, first derailing existing work begun by the DEP to study and prepare for the local effects of climate change and then vetoing a bipartisan bill meant to get the planning effort back on track.

LePage has often stated that diversifying Maine's energy sources and lowering electricity rates is a top priority for his administration, but he has made it clear that wind power is not part of those considerations. In speeches and public comments he has specifically pitted wind power against his preferred energy option: increased importation of hydroelectric power from Quebec.

"What I'm doing tonight is that I'm inviting all of you to come to my office in Augusta and we'll break big wind together," announced LePage to a Skowhegan Chamber of Commerce audience in April 2013 to laughter and applause. "We need to get the Maine people together and say why can't we get hydroelectricity instead of big wind power."

LePage repeated this mantra throughout his term despite evidence of decreasing wind power costs and the obvious unworkability of his hydro plan. Under provincial law, Quebec's low hydroelectric prices are reserved solely for the people of the province, and exported energy is sold at market rates. Even getting the power to Maine would require either a costly routing through New Brunswick or the building of an expensive and environmentally disruptive new transmission corridor through the western part of the state, likely making the electricity just as or more expensive than energy from other sources, including wind.

While playing the wind issue for laughs in public, LePage and his administration were working behind the scenes to insist on changes to a comprehensive energy deal being worked out in the legislature. Their amendments, which were eventually passed as a companion law, succeeded in sinking an already-approved deal with energy company StatOil to build Maine's first offshore wind installation. The move seemed directly contrary to LePage's usual rush to push aside regulations in order to encourage corporate investment, but he claimed that a project put forward by a consortium including the University of Maine and a number of more-local corporate partners would be better able to succeed without StatOil's competition.

Environmental advocates insist this reasoning was a smokescreen for LePage's anti-wind agenda, and LePage's own words seem to back them up. In the same speech in Skowhegan, LePage mocked the wind power pursuits of Maine's public universities, going so far as to falsely claim that a demonstration wind turbine at the University of Maine at Presque Isle was run by a "little electric motor" that turned the blades in order to trick people into thinking wind power works. This conspiracy theory once again garnered national headlines for Maine and its governor.

In May 2014, the University of Maine–led consortium lost out on a critical $47 million grant from the federal Department of Energy on which they had been depending to develop their turbines. Along with the loss of the Statoil investment, this development virtually guaranteed that Maine will not become the national leader on offshore wind that many had hoped, despite having the best offshore wind resources on the East Coast.

LePage's stance on clean energy isn't a clear-cut case of his ideological bent overpowering his corporate ties. After all, there are plenty of other companies in other industries that benefit from less wind power and less focus on climate change. But it does seem to be an area where he sheds his business-friendly image in favor of an ideology more acceptable to his activist base.

What has really separated climate change and wind power from other environmental issues isn't this shift in focus but the fact that they draw his personal attention at all. On the vast majority of environmental issues, LePage seems content to cede to lobbyists and corporations both policy development and the management of his staff.

chapter 8 Education

While running for governor, Paul LePage made his dissatisfaction with Maine's education system abundantly clear. In speeches, debates, and interviews, he said that education spending was too high and was wasted on too much administrative overhead, while results were poor and Maine's students were falling behind their counterparts across the country. He laid the blame for this disparity at the feet of school superintendents and the Maine Education Association (the MEA, Maine's teachers' union), which he said was using its political power to stifle reforms such as the implementation of private charter schools that could offer competition to public schools and force them to improve.

LePage often offered statistics to back up his assertions, although he rarely provided their sources. In a number of speeches during the election and since assuming office he said that Maine was fifth in the nation in per-student spending at $15,000 per pupil and was fiftieth among the states in "results," with only the District of Columbia doing worse. At other times he has used slightly different numbers, but he has always echoed the same sentiment, that Maine is spending too much for too little and it should be easy for a new governor to both save money and improve results.

LePage must have believed this rhetoric himself, because early in his first term he asked his hand-picked education commissioner to find $200 to $300 million worth of savings in education spending. He was probably surprised to learn in a memo he received in reply from Commissioner Stephen Bowen that even if administrative costs were cut by 25 percent, "which would be huge," according to Bowen, it would save the state only $15 million from a $2.1 billion education budget. Further significant cuts could not be accomplished simply through trimming fat, but would require closing schools, most likely small ones in rural areas according to the memo, which was obtained through a freedom of access request by the MEA.

"Pursuing a policy of somehow forcing schools to close, especially in the rural parts of the state that voted for you in part because they hated Baldacci's district consolidation mandate, would be politically very difficult to pull off," wrote Bowen to LePage.

Part of the reason that LePage's expectations were so wrong was that, as in a number of other issue areas, the numbers he had apparently believed and had consistently repeated during his campaign had little basis in reality. In that same memo, for instance, Bowen pegged annual average per-student spending at between $10,000 and $11,000 rather than the $15,000 LePage had claimed. Federal census data, calculated in a slightly different way, put Maine at $11,438 in per-student spending at the time, seventeenth in the nation and behind every other New England state, despite Maine's proportionally larger rural population.

Rather than last-in-the-nation outcomes, Maine students have also consistently scored well above average on the National Assessment of Educational Progress tests in reading, writing, mathematics, and science for the past decade.

Even after LePage gained office and had his own people telling him his numbers weren't right, however, he continued to use incorrect figures and added new false education anecdotes to his arsenal. During an August 2013 press conference, LePage claimed that Maine had such a terrible national academic reputation that the College of William and Mary in Virginia required Maine students attempting to enroll there to take a special aptitude test before they were considered for admission. No such requirement existed, of course, as dumbfounded William and Mary admissions staff quickly made clear.

In October 2013, almost three years after his election, LePage claimed while speaking to a conservative women's group in Falmouth that Maine's schools were so bad they were damaging the U.S. military's recruiting prospects in the state.

"This is the kicker, this is the most embarrassing one: only 25% of the kids who graduate high school in the state of Maine can qualify for the military," said LePage. "Fifty percent fall on academics and 25 percent fall on physical disabilities. Folks, 50 percent can't pass the test."

These statistics, once again, were completely wrong. The governor was perhaps confused by a report released by a group of retired generals, admirals, and other military commanders (an organization called Mission: Ready) intended to publicize the causes of ineligibility for military enlistment. The 75 percent number they reported was a reference not to Maine high school graduates but to all young adults across the country, and it was arrived at by calculating the number of young people nationwide who fail to graduate high school, the number with criminal records, and the effect of the nation's obesity problem on physical eligibility.

According to statistics released by Mission: Ready, only 19 percent of Maine graduates receive less-than-adequate scores on the military's academic aptitude tests, not the 50 percent LePage claimed. In reality, Maine students' rate

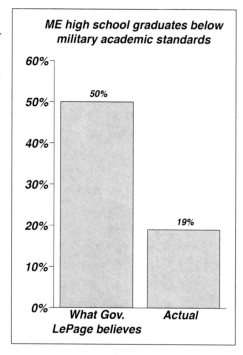

Figure 8.1. Nineteen percent of Maine high school graduates fail the military's academic aptitude tests, not the 50 percent claimed by LePage. Maine students perform substantially better than the national average.

of academic ineligibility was significantly lower than the national average.

Ironically, the top recommendation from these military leaders to improve eligibility rates is to increase access to early childhood education programs. Rather than follow this advice, LePage has cut or attempted to cut funding for Head Start, the pre-Kindergarten education program for low-income children, in every budget he has proposed. The program has been saved from a complete loss of state funding only through the repeated intervention of the legislature.

While repeating these and other false statistics to claim that Maine public schools aren't performing as they should, LePage has also been pushing to allow more public money to flow out of Maine's public school system and into private charter and virtual schools. Charter school legislation backed by LePage and passed in 2011 allows new charter schools to be founded in Maine and also allows public funds to be spent on educating students through online classes at virtual academies.

The LePage administration's push for virtual schools is one of the most well-documented aspects of his time in office, thanks to Freedom of Access requests by Public Interest and the Maine Education Association and, again, the work of investigative journalist Colin Woodard. In 2012, Woodard won a George Polk award for a series of articles published in the *Maine Sunday Telegram* showing how corporate interests heavily influenced the LePage administration's education policies, particularly his push for public funding of virtual charter schools.

LePage's ties to virtual education companies began during his campaign when K12 Education, the nation's largest online education management organization, gave $19,000 to the Republican Governors Association's Maine PAC (political action committee), money that was then spent helping LePage win the general election.

Once in office, LePage selected Bowen, a hard-hitting conservative school privatization advocate who worked for the Maine Heritage Policy Center, to serve as his education commissioner. Bowen initially turned down the post, preferring to work strictly on policy, but later accepted after LePage said he couldn't find anyone else he trusted who was willing to run the department.

Soon after assuming the post, Bowen reached out to education policy staff from Jeb Bush's Foundation for Excellence in Education (FEE) in Florida, a pro-virtual schools policy think tank that receives funding from K12 and another large virtual schools company, Connections Education. Bowen also worked with the same two companies through his membership in the American Legislative Exchange Council. As a member of ALEC's education committee until at least March 2011, Bowen collaborated with representatives from Connections and K12 to draft model legislation on virtual schools. Mickey Revenaugh, senior vice president of state relations for Connections Education, served as chair of the committee.

By pulling the strings of this web of corporate and political connections to Bowen and LePage, K12 got exactly what it wanted in Maine—a doorway through which to enter the state and sell its for-profit virtual charter schools. Maine was a particularly enticing marketplace for the company due to the Maine Learning Technology Initiative, a policy implemented by former governor Angus King that continues to provide all seventh- and eighth-grade students in Maine's public schools with laptop computers.

In the states where they have been legalized, K12's online schools have made the company a steady profit from diverted public education funds and have often delivered a sub-par educational product to the students they are meant to serve. An investigation in Florida in 2011 found that students were not being taught by certified instructors as required by state law and that licensed teachers had been pressured to lie on official forms in order to cover up the company's fraudulent practices.

In addition to taking advantage of their links to LePage, the virtual school companies also targeted the Republican legislature, with K12 alone spending $33,074 on lobbying in Maine in 2011 in order to help ensure the passage of the charter school legislation. The bill did pass the Republican legislature, but with a provision attached requiring virtual schools wishing to operate in the state to be governed by a local nonprofit organization. LePage signed the bill and then went a step further, issuing an executive order outlining a ten-point plan for future virtual education in Maine.

Among other provisions, the order called for an end to regulation of virtual school student-to-teacher ratios, full public per-pupil funding of online schools, the removal of local school board choice in allowing or prohibiting online courses, and the striking down of any state regulations that might limit the reach of virtual schools or assess "inputs such as teacher certification, programmatic budgets and textbook reviews." It was later revealed by Woodard's reporting that the order LePage issued was written almost entirely by the K12-funded policy staff at Jeb Bush's think tank.

Even with all the forward momentum provided by the LePage administration and with a cooperative Republican-controlled legislature and lobbying dollars smoothing the way, the gravy train of public funds was derailed before it could make it to the private virtual school companies thanks to the Maine Charter School Commission, a public board created by the legislation that LePage had championed.

The commission is a seven-member panel appointed by the Maine Board of Education (which is in turn appointed by the governor) and tasked with reviewing applications for new charter schools, including those from the local nonprofits associated with K12 and Connections. The commission found that both organizations were basically hollow shells created by the virtual school companies and did not meet the law's requirements for local control.

The K12-affiliated group, Maine Virtual Academy, was helmed by former LePage primary rival Peter Mills, whom LePage had since appointed to head the Maine Turnpike Authority. After being aproached by K12, Mills helped to put together a charter board to submit a proposal on their behalf. The document they submitted would have delegated all day-to-day management decisions to officials selected by K12 and allowed the Virginia-based company to make all final hiring and supervisory decisions for the academy, basically giving K12 free rein and a blank check.

The Connections-affiliated virtual charter application was presented on behalf of a board that included Tea Party-backed State Representative Amy Volk, then-State GOP Vice Chair Ruth Summers, and Maine Americans for Prosperity head Carol Weston. Weston is a former state senator and was ALEC's "state legislator of the year" in 2008. The commission found similar issues with their application, suggesting that the company was really running the show and that the board members were there more as figureheads.

LePage responded quickly and angrily to the commission's decision to hold the two applications for review, holding two press conferences on the same day to publicly excoriate the commission and its members.

"I am asking them for the good of the kids of the state of Maine, please go away. We need some people with backbones," said LePage.

The governor also once again claimed that Maine schools were failing and cited the same false statistics about per-student spending and educational outcomes. Despite the rhetoric, the board held firm and the applications were rescinded. It wasn't until March 2014 that they were again reviewed by the board, and this time the Connections-linked application was approved. K12's school proposal was once again rejected.

Also in 2014, the Maine Legislature passed a bill to create a state-run virtual public charter school, seeking to provide the distance learning benefits of an online school while avoiding the problems for-profit academies had encountered in other states. The legislation would also have placed a temporary moratorium on for-profit virtual charters. The bill was vetoed by LePage.

The media attention to the virtual schools issue made it more difficult for corporate education interests to influence policy quite as blatantly as they had done initially, and the change in control of the state legislature in 2013, following an election fought in part on the issue of public money being diverted to private schools, left LePage less able to pass new legislation on the issue.

As the LePage administration shifted its focus away from outright implementation of private and virtual schools, it turned toward a more subtle initiative to undermine public education. In February 2013, during his annual State of the State address, LePage announced that he would begin issuing A–F grades for public schools. When he released the grades that May, it quickly became clear that they were based almost entirely on the schools' aggregate standardized test scores in just two subjects, math and reading, and were designed to allow his administration to classify a certain number of public schools as "failing."

In this fight, LePage sought political enemies who were easier to attack than the nonpartisan charter school board–mainly the Maine Education Association–and he seemed to relish the prospect of a public fight with the union.

"If you think I've caused trouble lately, you wait in the next couple weeks when the grades on all the schools come out," said LePage in an address to the Skowhegan Chamber of Commerce in April 2013. "I will guarantee you that you will see the most vicious education campaign ads that you've ever seen in your life next year, because I am going to be the next Scott Walker in this country, because I am challenging the status quo."

This kind of rhetoric was vintage LePage, but the specifics of the policy he was advancing were surprising, especially for those who were familiar with his expressed views on educational evaluation to that point. Throughout his campaign and for the first two years of his tenure in office, LePage had loudly and consistently railed against what he called "teaching to the test."

"It robs our children of classroom time," he said of standardized assessments to a Tea Party audience at a campaign event in 2010.

"We need to eliminate teaching to national assessments and allow teachers to create a learning environment that challenges all of our students to excel to their own diverse strengths rather than a standard of mediocrity," read his campaign website during the general election.

In 2011, addressing the Maine Symposium on Higher Education, LePage noted that he himself earned less than a 300 when he first took the SATs in English. "It's never been about grades," said LePage. "It's about effort."

But something had changed in 2013. LePage's major new policy initiative was much more about grades than effort.

Because LePage's A–F evaluation was based almost entirely on standardized test scores, which correlate closely with poverty levels, the grades for each school were predictable: Schools in rich areas did well on LePage's measure of assessment, and those in poor areas did poorly.

The grades were also curved rather than being measured against some national or independent benchmark, guaranteeing at the outset that a large number of schools would receive failing grades.

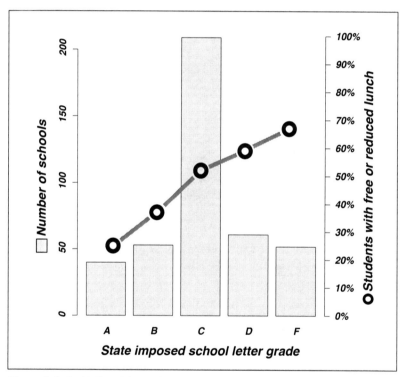

Figure 8.2. In 2013 and 2014, the LePage administration gave letter grades to Maine's elementary schools based on each school's aggregate performance on standardized tests in English and math. In both years (2013 shown here), performance tracked closely with school-district poverty as measured by the percentage of students receiving subsidized lunches. Schools in poor communities do poorly. The shaded bars show the number of schools receiving each letter grade.

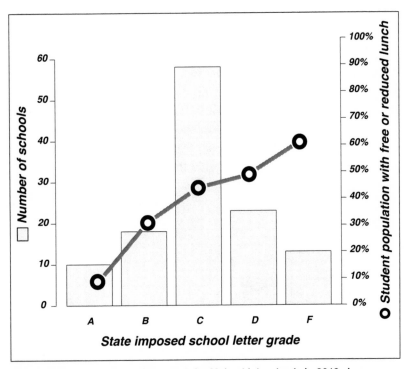

Figure 8.3. The corresponding graph for Maine high schools in 2013 shows a similar result.

The link between income and standardized test results is well known and well examined. One study from Washington State, for instance, found that 80 percent of the variance in college entrance exams can be explained by parental income levels alone. A Harvard experiment in which poor families were given additional income and all other factors were held equal found that children's test scores radically improved. What this means in the context of LePage's grades is that there's very little room for so-called failing schools to maneuver. Basically, the only way for schools to significantly improve their results in the face of demographic difficulties would be for teachers to shift their focus to "teaching to the tests" in an attempt to game the system, exactly what LePage had once railed against. This dynamic was compounded by a quirk in LePage's assessments that gave wealthy schools with high scores more credit for maintaining their results than it did to lower-ranked schools for improving theirs.

So why assign grades that told people what they already knew? Why grade on an arbitrary curve, thus guaranteeing that most poor districts would fare poorly? Why the sudden about-face on standardized testing? The answers may have been inadvertently revealed in an e-mail exchange between Bowen and the governor's staff on the topic of "school accountability."

"Accountability is a good issue politically, I think," wrote Bowen in an e-mail to the governor. He noted that they could use the grading system to make a case for state takeover of schools or "to allow students in failing schools to have school choice." "School choice" is well-established code for the use of public money for private and charter schools.

In 2014, *U.S. News and World Report* released state-by-state rankings of U.S. high schools. In contrast with the high percentage of failing schools that LePage's grades had indicated, the report showed Maine tied with California as first in the nation for the highest percentage of high schools earning top marks.

Most of LePage's attempted education policy reforms were both corporate-friendly and Tea Party–approved. His proposals to weaken public education, for instance, had the potential of directly benefiting both for-profit education firms and parents who homeschool their children, an important group within the Tea Party movement. Education policy, however, also constituted one of the biggest showdowns between business interests and Tea Party activists during his term, and the way in which LePage handled it gives some insight into his broader approach to balancing the interests of his two most important constituencies.

The Common Core State Standards are a set of measures of assessment meant to coordinate and raise expectations for primary and secondary student learning across the country, better preparing students for higher education and employment. The standards were developed not by the federal government but by a voluntary collaboration of all fifty states through the National Governors

Association and the Council of Chief State School Officers. The state of Maine joined the Common Core initiative under the Baldacci administration, and the standards themselves were adopted in 2011 when LePage signed a bill that had been submitted on behalf of the Department of Education and passed by the Republican-controlled legislature.

In the minds of some Tea Party activists, however, Common Core (or "Obamacore," or "Commie Core" as they sometimes refer to it) is at the very least an example of too much centralization and standardization of education and at worst an unconstitutional attempt by the federal government (or, in the imaginations of some, the United Nations) to indoctrinate the nation's children for insidious purposes. Right-wing radio host Glenn Beck has claimed that the initiative is a dragnet for personal student data meant to allow the government to monitor each child and control their future so that they "will be a cog in the machine forever."

This anti-Common Core activism has prompted Tea Party-friendly governors in several states to reject the standards. Texas Governor Rick Perry even called in to Glenn Beck's show to denounce the standards.

Governor LePage and Commissioner Bowen both originally supported Maine's adoption of the Common Core standards, and when the governor signed the bill changing state regulations to conform to Common Core, the Department of Education sent out a celebratory press release.

"Adopting the standards means Maine teachers will have a clear set of standards to work with, and will be able to tailor their teaching to the new, rigorous expectations of what students should know and be able to do," read the release.

"As I've been traveling around the state, I have heard it over and over from teachers—they want us to adopt the Common Core," Bowen was quoted as saying.

As opposition to the standards from the conservative right—including the Maine Heritage Policy Center, Bowen's former employer—intensified, however, the two men's opinions seemed to diverge. While Bowen maintained his public support for the standards and the Department of Education continued to send out press releases with titles like "Business Leaders Support Common Core Standards," as they did in 2013, LePage began to try to distance himself from Common Core.

In June 2012, Bowen wrote a memo to LePage saying that he had heard from the governor's staff that LePage now had reservations about the standards. The commissioner wrote that he was surprised to learn they weren't on the same page and asked to meet with the governor soon to set things straight.

In September 2013, LePage issued an executive order specifically declaring that the state "shall not adopt any educational standards, curricula or instructional approaches that may be mandated by the federal government." His order said the state would also refuse to turn over any personal student data. On the surface this might seem to be a rejection of Common Core, but the order didn't actually change anything about the state's approach to public education.

"The order amounts to a transparent attempt by LePage to shore up support among members of his conservative base who are wary of any federal government intervention into education. At the same time, the order is written so as to have virtually no effect on the state's education policy and programs," editorialized the *Bangor Daily News* at the time.

LePage was walking a difficult line between the work and stated opinions of his own administration and the growing fear and anger of his base. In public he mostly managed to walk the line well, but in at least one Tea Party gathering, he stumbled.

"First of all, the law that we committed to was passed in the 124th Legislature. It was under Baldacci, it was not under Governor LePage," LePage falsely claimed in a speech to the Informed Women's Network (the same event at which he claimed that Maine's schools were failing to meet military standards).

"I'm telling you there's no state standard. I haven't allowed it out. So if they're telling you that, I don't know where they're getting it. There is no such thing as a state standard that has been sent out to the schools," LePage continued when asked by one of the group's members about their own children's school's preparations for testing based on Common Core.

LePage was lying to the group. Not only had there been a Common Core–based state standard in place for more than two years at that point, but the state had also since signed on to the Smarter Balanced Assessments, standardized tests based on those standards that were set to be administered to Maine students the following school year. His administration had begun sending information about the tests to schools in June 2013.

When this fact was pointed out to LePage, however, he denied that the test or the standards existed at all.

"I am there every single day and I am telling you that what they're telling you is not coming from the state. I'm there every single day," said LePage. "It does not exist, folks."

Either the governor didn't know about some of the most high-profile work of his own Education Department, or he was attempting to obfuscate the truth in order to tamp down unrest among his base. It was a bit of a turnabout for the governor; in the past, most of his false policy statements had been made in order to rile up Tea Party groups, not to placate them.

Bowen resigned from the LePage administration a week after the governor signed his executive order disavowing Common Core and took a job as the director of innovation for the Council of Chief State School Officers, one of the groups that had created the standards.

Except for their late disagreement over Common Core, Bowen and the governor had mostly been in ideological harmony on education policy, although their correspondence reveals that they'd had some disagreements about how exactly to push their reforms. In one e-mail to LePage education advisor Jonathan Nass, Bowen noted that there was a risk in an upcoming meeting with the governor "that he yells at us/me again."

In another set of e-mails that caused embarrassment to the administration when made public, Bowen objected to LePage's attempt to hire Ashley Marble, Maine's entrant in the 2011 Miss USA pageant, as a public ambassador for technical education, declaring that a "beauty queen with, from what I can tell, no CTE knowledge or background" would never be hired by the DOE on his watch.

"You guys know I'm a team player and I'm working 80 hours a week to get [a] constantly shifting education agenda put together," Bowen wrote. "No way I'm doing this, though. Absolutely no way."

LePage apparently backed down in that instance, and Marble was not given a position in the department.

As is true in several areas of policy, the governor's public fights and colorful language aren't the aspects of his tenure that will have the most lasting effect on Maine's education system. In fact, LePage's greatest legacy in the field of education likely won't even be the implementation of Common Core or the establishment of virtual schools, but will stem from the overall decrease in funding to Maine's schools during his governorship.

While LePage often claims that he slightly increased K-12 funding in his first budget, this ignores the fact that temporary federal stimulus funding had previously been picking up some of the slack. Overall, his budgets have represented a sharp decrease in funding, and the burden of these cuts has fallen on Maine educators and students. A study commissioned by the legislature found that while the state was paying more than 50 percent of the cost of education in the 2008-2009 school year, the state share had dropped to 42 percent by 2013. According to DOE figures, from 2008 to 2013, direct state funding to schools decreased by $110 million.

LePage's attempts to cut ancillary education programs such as Head Start, his policies of diverting public money to private schools, and his cuts to municipal revenue sharing, potentially forcing towns to cut back on their own education spending, may further exacerbate his administration's direct cuts in education spending. Together they represent a significant failure to invest in Maine children that will likely have continuing repercussions for the future of the state.

chapter 9 Taxes and Budgets

In a 2013 interview with reporter John Christie of the Maine Center for Public Interest Reporting, and again later that year at a meeting of the Informed Women's Network, Governor LePage made an argument for cutting taxes for the wealthy based on a millionaire gap he claimed was growing with neighboring New Hampshire.

"Twenty-five years ago Maine had about 2,000 millionaires. Maine has 400 now. New Hampshire at the time had about 500, right now they have 4,000. That's the difference. That's when you talk about prosperity and you talk about building an economy those are the things that you need to concern yourself with. So, I am looking at taxation as a big issue," said LePage at the event.

There are no solid state-by-state data on the total number of millionaires. Even the IRS tracking of tax returns over $1 million only goes back to 1997. However, even if LePage had somehow managed to access the bank and investment accounts of everyone in New England, there's no way that his numbers are accurate.

In fact, IRS data show Maine gaining the superwealthy at a faster rate than New Hampshire, despite differences in tax rates and despite New Hampshire's proximity to Boston. In Maine there were 307 million-dollar-plus tax returns in 1997 and 562 in 2011, an 83 percent increase. In New Hampshire there were 683 in 1997 and 1,124 in 2011, a 64 percent increase. (See Figure 9.1.)

In addition, the nonprofit Tax Foundation's tracking of inter-migration between New Hampshire and Maine from 1993 to 2010 shows that, rather than losing population to New Hampshire over that period, Maine netted 1,361 people who used to file returns in the

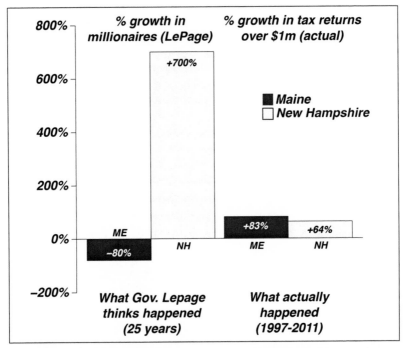

Figure 9.1. LePage's assessment of the trend in millionaires in Maine and New Hampshire versus reality.

neighboring state, resulting in a net increase in adjusted gross income of $164,022,000. People who moved from New Hampshire to Maine were also slightly wealthier (average incomes of $39,41) than those who moved in the other direction (average incomes of $36,752).

While LePage's figures were once again false, his quotes pointed toward a greater truth. As his statement indicates and as his policies have shown, LePage's major concern on the issue of taxes is their effect on the wealthy.

In 2011, in his first budget, Governor LePage proposed one of the greatest transfers of wealth in Maine history. The budget included a significant cut to the state income tax, reducing the top tax rate from 8.5 to 7.95 percent. It also doubled the exemption for the estate tax to $2 million, saving about 550 of the wealthiest families in Maine $30 million a year on their inheritances. In total, the Maine Center for

Economic Policy (MECEP) calculated that the cuts created a budget gap of $203 million in the first two years of its effect and $443 million over the next two. (See also Figure 14.3.)

To fill this gap, LePage proposed pension cuts for state employees and teachers, cuts to public assistance programs that would predominantly affect immigrants and people with disabilities, property tax increases, cuts to funding for education, and cuts to state health care and prescription drug programs for the poor and elderly.

The Republican-controlled legislature passed most of LePage's proposals into law. Some of the most draconian measures, including cutting MaineCare (Maine's version of Medicaid) coverage for 28,000 residents and eliminating the state's Low Cost Drugs for the Elderly and Disabled Program (DEL), were removed from the initial budget in a compromise with minority Democrats in order to reach a two-thirds legislative majority to pass the bill, but most of them were put right back into effect in LePage's supplemental budget passed the next year on a party-line vote.

The property tax increases in that first budget came mostly in the form of the elimination of the Maine circuit breaker program, meant to alleviate property tax burdens for low- and middle-income Mainers, and its replacement with a credit that saw homeowners reimbursed at a far lower rate. For someone making the state's minimum wage, these changes meant a possible $5 decrease in income taxes for the year but a likely $400 increase in property taxes. For the top 1 percent of income earners, on the other hand, overall taxes dropped an average of almost $3,000. (See also Figures 14.4 and 14.5.)

LePage often talks about the tax cuts as if they were a boon for the poor and middle class, citing the fact that 70,000 low-income Mainers saw their income tax liability disappear completely under his plan. He fails to mention, however, that the average income tax reduction for this group was only $7, and that his tax policies would end up costing almost all of them far more than that in the long run. The real benefits of his plan accrued to the wealthy.

MECEP estimated that with the tax changes, including higher local property taxes as a result of cuts in funding to municipalities, the bottom 40 percent of Maine income earners saw a tax increase because of LePage's first budget, rather than a cut, and that's not counting the deficits the tax cuts caused in subsequent budgets, leading to more cuts and magnifying this divergent effect. (See Figure 14.5.)

Republicans also passed another law, yet to have any real impact, that automatically applies future state budget surplus funds (even temporary ones) toward permanently reducing the state income tax rate to a target of 4.0 percent, severely restricting the state's ability to put money away or invest in the future. LePage has said he would like to eliminate the state income tax completely, despite the fact that this tax is far more progressive (being based on people's actual income) than sales and property taxes.

This transfer of wealth from those who can least afford to lose it to those having the least need for it has not gone unnoticed. The tax breaks and program cuts included in LePage's first budget became a central issue of the 2012 election, with both parties hammering away at it. Republicans lauded the largest tax cut in Maine history, while Democrats attacked their opponents for supporting the new tax breaks that predominantly benefited the rich.

A *Bangor Daily News* reporter's cataloging of mailers received by one household in one of the most hotly contested senate districts offers a good overview of the focus and tenor of the 2012 races. Mail sent on behalf of Republican incumbent Senator Nichi Farnham lampooned her opponent, medical doctor Geoff Gratwick, for having voted for local tax increases as a member of the city council, declaring him to be "Dr. Taxes." The Democrats' most prominent policy attack on Farnham was that she had voted for "tax breaks for the rich." There were other important election issues, including health care and education, but some of the most central messages from both sides were on taxes.

The same was true in senate and house districts across the state. Republicans continued a strategy that had been successful for them in the past of painting their opponents as tax-and-spend liberals. (In 2010, they had bought ads accusing Democrats of passing a "tax on babies" by implementing a new fee on medical procedures.)

Meanwhile, Democrats tapped into new arguments about inequality and tax fairness, messages that fit well with the themes of the national presidential election in 2012 and the increased focus on disparity engendered by the Occupy Wall Street movement.

The Democrats' message of fairness apparently worked far better than the Republicans' message of lower taxes, and on Election Day 2012, Democrats won by wide margins across the state, reclaiming both chambers from the Republicans. Almost every Republican incumbent in a vulnerable district went down to defeat.

Record spending on both sides was boosted by a U.S. Supreme Court ruling that had struck down portions of Maine's Clean Elections law and made it easier for outside groups to influence elections. In part because of this cash infusion, the legislative elections that year had a higher profile than normal, and both sides had enough resources to get their messages on taxes out to voters during the campaign, even in the midst of a national presidential contest.

LePage's first biennial budget was all about passing his new tax cuts, but his second budget, proposed in January 2013, was all about preserving them from the mandate for repeal that newly elected Democrats felt they had won. LePage instead proposed filling the new budget gap caused as the tax cuts came into full effect with additional service cuts and the elimination of the state's revenue sharing with Maine municipalities.

Revenue-sharing funds are an important part of town budgets in Maine. With limited alternative revenue options at the municipal level, cuts in this transfer from the state can either be made up by an increase in local property taxes or absorbed by cuts to local schools and municipal services. There are no other real alternatives. In addition to these indirect tax increases, LePage's budget proposal also advocated raising property taxes directly by further cutting back on property tax relief programs.

Governor LePage argued that the towns did not need to raise taxes or cut services and could instead trim fat from municipal budgets. His argument was somewhat undercut, however, when a video recording emerged of him speaking at a Waterville City Council meeting during his time as mayor. The video captures Mayor LePage angrily attacking state government for exactly the same kind of revenue-sharing cuts that, as governor, he now proposed. At the time, LePage promised they would lead to property tax increases.

This focus on cuts to towns was a new tactic by the governor, who until this point had insisted that there was plenty of wasteful spending at the state level that could be pared back. In attempting instead to pass the buck to a different level of government, LePage was in essence admitting that state expenditures were already as efficient as possible.

"[B]y the governor's own admission, there is nothing left to cut," editorialized the *Portland Press Herald*.

When Democrats proposed rescinding LePage's tax breaks to fill the budget gap as a way of preventing the property tax increases, it sparked a debate over progressivity in taxation.

Property taxes, along with certain sales taxes, are among the most regressive forms of taxation. The poor, who spend a higher portion of their income on basic necessities such as food and shelter, are hit harder than wealthier individuals when taxes on those necessities are increased. Income taxes, on the other hand, represent one of the most progressive forms of taxation, especially when tiered so that those who make more pay a higher rate. (See Figure 14.4.)

In the end, the two sides found a compromise that neither particularly liked but that both parties in the legislature, at least, could live with. Revenue sharing would be cut, but not as much as LePage had proposed. The governor's income and estate tax cuts would remain in place, and some sales taxes would be raised to make up the difference. Some of the increase was regressive and across the board, while other tax increases on food and lodging were meant to predominantly affect tourists rather than Maine residents. A task force was formed to identify a number of corporate tax loopholes that could be closed to balance the budget, and the LePage administration was tasked with finding program efficiencies to save an additional $30 million.

Despite getting part of what he wanted on revenue sharing and all of what he wanted on the income and estate tax cuts, LePage stridently opposed the budget deal. He vetoed the compromise bill and lobbied Republican legislators to uphold his veto, a move that, if successful, would have caused a government shutdown. Republican legislators, unwilling to be responsible for bringing state government to a halt, instead did something they had done only four other times to that point (despite LePage's record eighty-three vetoes) and voted to uphold the bill. It won the two-thirds majority needed to become law over the governor's objections.

Unlike national Tea Party–backed Republican politicians, who in 2013 proved more than willing to shut down the federal government over the debt ceiling, enough Maine GOP legislators chose to compromise in order to keep the state government functioning.

LePage was livid. He railed against his fellow Republicans for what he saw as a betrayal of conservative values, declaring at a press conference that, while the state had taken two steps forward with his first budget, with this one they had taken three steps back.

"I will say this: The Republican Party is not a very strong one," said LePage. When a reporter asked why he wasn't at least pleased that his tax cuts had been preserved, LePage insisted that "we didn't save anything," and that if they had been repealed, regular Mainers would have risen up in protest and ensured "a massive Republican win" in the next election.

After failing to get his way, LePage essentially decided to wash his hands of the whole affair. Instead of drafting a supplemental budget for 2014, a step the governor normally takes in order to account for new expense and revenue forecasts, he took the unprecedented step of refusing to submit any new budget legislation, telling the legislature that it was now up to them to figure things out on their own.

"They overrode my veto, and therefore they have inherited this budget and they need to figure out a way to balance it," LePage told the *Lewiston Sun Journal.*

LePage's disengagement ultimately helped allow the passage of one of the more progressive, humane budget supplements in recent years. In 2014, majority Democrats in the legislature were able to repeal LePage's revenue-sharing cuts, increase funding for health care and education, and even raise some taxes on corporations and the wealthy. The supplemental budget was rejected by LePage, but a majority of Republicans joined Democrats in overriding his veto.

In total, LePage's tax policies have been a boon for the richest individuals and families in the state and have come at the expense of programs serving some of Maine's neediest. They have also led to net tax increases for many of those who can least afford them. The impact of these policies on the economy will be examined briefly in Chapter 14, but it has not been positive.

Even an election that was fought on taxes and that Republicans resoundingly lost didn't dull LePage's ardor for more tax breaks and program cuts. The election did prove, however, that LePage's stalwart Tea Party supporters didn't have the electoral muscle to defend the conservative majorities won in 2010 in a presidential election year. The debate is continuing in 2014, and the legacy of LePage's tax policy will be a central, contentious topic as he seeks to mobilize enough of that support to win reelection.

chapter 10 Health Care

Despite the timing of the national debate on President Barack Obama's Affordable Care Act (labeled "Obamacare" by its detractors, a moniker the president was happy to claim)–a debate that fed the strength of the Tea Party in 2010–health care was never a core issue of Paul LePage's campaign for governor. When he addressed the subject, it was usually to lambaste Obamacare as unconstitutional or to lump the government's spending on MaineCare (Maine's version of Medicaid) with his complaints about welfare expenditures and the effects of such support on Mainers' work ethics and moral fiber.

On a few occasions, usually when asked about it by a reporter or member of the audience at an event, he also blasted his predecessor's attempt to implement a program called Dirigo Health, which was meant to offer premium subsidies for small businesses and low-income individuals. He offered almost no new health care policy prescriptions of his own.

Health care policy, however, has become a major focus of LePage's governorship. In 2011 and 2012 there was a contentious debate over a package of conservative, market-based health care reforms pushed and eventually passed by the Republican-controlled legislature, while 2013 and 2014 brought a showdown between LePage and the legislature (by then Democratically controlled) on how best to make debt repayments to Maine's hospitals and whether to accept federal funding made available through the Affordable Care Act to expand health care coverage.

The Republican health care reform law proved to be one of the most divisive pieces of legislation passed in the 125th Legislature.

Dubbed the "rate hike bill" by opponents for its effects on insurance premiums through a wide swath of the state, the law became one of the most visible issues during the 2012 election, in which Republicans lost their legislative majorities by wide margins.

The regulatory changes for the individual and small business markets proposed by Republicans as part of their 2011 reform package were mostly ideas that had long been championed by insurance companies and by conservative groups including the Maine Heritage Policy Center. They included abandoning regulations that had prohibited insurers from charging different rates based on age and geography, eliminating public rate-review hearings for premium increases on certain insurance products, and allowing health insurance to be purchased across state lines from other New England states (presumably those with even fewer consumer protections). Vermont, which was beginning to implement a single-payer health care system, was excluded from the list of acceptable states from which Mainers could purchase insurance. The bill also implemented a new $4-per-month tax on insurance premiums, paid into a fund to reimburse insurance companies.

Unlike most legislation, which is preceded by months of hearings, work sessions, and opportunities for debate and amendment, the insurance reform bill was drafted, reported out of the Insurance and Financial Services Committee, passed by the legislature, and signed by Governor LePage in a matter of days. Perhaps knowing the issue would be a difficult one to win in a long war of attrition, LePage and Republican leaders in the house and senate opted for a tactical strike and displayed a purposeful coordination between the branches of government to a degree they managed on few other issues.

At the center of the bill's quick progress through the legislature was Tarren Bragdon, the executive director of the Maine Heritage Policy Center (MHPC) and one of the three co-chairs of Governor LePage's official transition team. Bragdon helped to write the legislation and then shepherded Republicans on the committee through the process of striking four pages of legislative language from an existing bill that had already had a public hearing and replacing the deleted material with forty-five new pages of policy. The bill was then exempted from fiscal review by the Appropriations Committee, a contentious move that prompted Republican House Appropriations Chair Pat Flood to resign his post in protest. It eventually passed both houses on mostly party-line votes.

Insurance companies, a powerful political bloc and perhaps the biggest beneficiaries of the relaxed regulations, lobbied heavily on the legislation. In addition, a report released by the Maine Center for Clean Elections found that the state's largest health insurance company, Anthem, significantly changed its political giving patterns in the months just before and after the legislation was proposed and passed. Whereas in past cycles Anthem's money had flowed at roughly equal rates to candidates and PACs on both sides of the aisle, in 2010 the company, a subsidiary of national insurance giant Well-Point, switched to giving 84 percent of its contributions to Republicans. The Maine Republican Party was by far the largest recipient, and this pattern of giving continued during and after the debate over the regulatory changes.

The speed of the legislation's passage may have been hastened by a speech Governor LePage had given the month before at a breakfast hosted by the Androscoggin County Chamber of Commerce. LePage complained angrily that the legislature "hadn't done a damn thing" so far, and he gave both the Republican-controlled legislature and his own administration a grade of "F" for not having accomplished enough of his goals. The speech followed the publication of a letter written by eight Republican state senators who blamed LePage's controversial statements and attitude for making progress difficult in Augusta.

The scope of the legislation and the speed with which it was passed prompted a backlash from Democratic legislators and health care advocates, who bristled at what they saw as a handout to insurance companies and at the lack of the usual democratic processes to air concerns and improve the proposed legislation. Representatives had to pass through a gauntlet of protesters in the State House hallways in order to take their final votes on the bill. A *Bangor Daily News* editorial called the process "a lesson in how not to lead."

During the boisterous debate over the health insurance reform bill, Republican supporters made a number of promises about the effects of the legislation. They publicly guaranteed that not only would insurance costs decrease for young urban populations, but that fewer regulations and increased competition among insurance providers would lead to decreased costs for everyone.

"Lower rates for all" was the headline of an opinion piece written by MHPC board member Joel Allenbaugh, who at the same time was working as a lobbyist for a group funded by insurance companies.

Removing the regulations "will lower prices for younger people, not raise them for older people," declared Representative Jonathan McKane, a member of the Insurance and Financial Services Committee and one of the main proponents of the Republican plan.

On a YouTube video released by senate Republicans, Senate Insurance and Financial Services chair Rodney Whittemore directly addressed the question of whether some Mainers might end up paying more, saying, "Not at all. As a matter of fact I would be probably surprised if their costs didn't go down."

Within a year of passage of the bill, and despite proponents' claims, it became obvious that rates were going up for a substantial number of Mainers, especially small business owners. While some young, healthy, urban Mainers did see premiums decrease, costs skyrocketed in rural Maine as insurance companies took advantage of the law's new leniency on price discrimination. Ninety percent of small businesses statewide were hit with higher premiums, and some businesses with older employees in rural areas saw their rates more than double in just a few months' time. Those hit the hardest lived mostly in the areas of the state that had voted to give the Republicans their majorities and elect LePage governor just two years earlier.

The rate hikes became an albatross around the neck of Republican state legislators in rural districts in the 2012 election, at least as much as the tax cuts for the wealthy, especially since the premium increases had an outsized impact among the key voting blocs of small business owners and middle-aged and elderly Mainers. Maine Republican candidates continued to receive significant financial support from Anthem, including indirectly through outlays from the national Republican State Leadership Committee, but it wasn't enough to stem the bleeding. The Maine House and Senate both flipped to Democratic control in the election.

In 2013 the new Democratic legislature passed bills to rein in the worst excesses of the insurance reforms, but they were vetoed by LePage. Some of the law's provisions were eventually superseded by protections in the Affordable Care Act.

While the 2011 insurance reforms were mostly championed by Republican legislators and MHPC, with LePage and his administration playing an important but secondary role, the governor was front and center for the next big health care debate.

It hasn't always been his main focus, but LePage has made his distaste for the Affordable Care Act clear from the beginning of his first campaign, calling it unconstitutional and saying that one of his first acts as governor would be to urge Maine's attorney general to challenge the law. When the U.S. Supreme Court upheld its legality, LePage responded with one of the most controversial statements of his career. On July 8, 2012, LePage used his weekly radio address to vow that he would do everything he could to stymie the law's implementation, calling the IRS "the new Gestapo" for the agency's role in helping to implement portions of the law.

Unlike many of LePage's colorful or controversial comments, which have been made off-the-cuff or in front of small audiences of political allies, this reference to the Nazis' secret-police force was part of an official, vetted communication released by his office. According to administration communications director Adrienne Bennett, LePage insisted the line be inserted into his prepared remarks.

After the Anti-Defamation League and others called for LePage to disavow the comment, the governor issued a statement lamenting that "the word *Gestapo* has clouded my message." Speaking to a reporter in Vermont a week later, however, LePage doubled down on the sentiment of his statement, acknowledging that the gestapo had "killed a lot of people" but insisting that the IRS was "headed in that direction."

Although it received less attention than his Gestapo comment, another portion of that radio address may have a more lasting impact: the announcement that the LePage administration would refuse to accept federal funds to expand MaineCare to cover those making less than 133 percent of the federal poverty level. As part of this policy, LePage would also continue the removal of MaineCare coverage for many residents cut from the program in his budget and for whom coverage could be extended with the acceptance of federal funds.

The debate over MaineCare expansion became a central point of contention first in the 2013 legislative sessions and again in the 2014 session. In 2013 a coalition of Democrats and moderate Republicans passed a bill allowing the expansion and then, after the bill was vetoed by LePage, came within two votes in the house of securing the two-thirds majority necessary to override the governor's veto.

For a time, accepting federal funds became intertwined with another health care issue–the final repayment of money owed to Maine's hospitals.

The hospital debt issue is one that LePage played masterfully, and it's a lesson in how well his political skills and instincts can work, given the right circumstances.

The issue itself was relatively straightforward: The state had owed Maine hospitals money for a number of years due to underestimates of health care costs. The administration of Democratic Governor John Baldacci and previous legislatures had taken on the task of paying off the debts and had mostly settled them. In 2009 they had also begun the switch to a pay-as-you-go system that ensured no more debt would be accrued. The last portion of the debt, totaling almost $500 million (of which the state was responsible for less than $200 million, thanks to a federal match), was still unpaid as LePage took office.

During his first two years in office, LePage made a small payment on the hospital debt but didn't settle the full amount, choosing to focus instead on other priorities, including his income and estate tax cuts. Starting just before the 2012 election and continuing through the first session of the next legislature, however, LePage declared the issue to be a moral imperative and his administration's top priority.

LePage's plan for repayment was revealed in an unusual way. In August 2012, speaking to a Republican audience at the Sea Dog restaurant in Bangor, he confided that he was planning to interrupt the reelection campaigns of Republican incumbents to call them back to Augusta for a special legislative session. LePage refused to say what policy he was planning to propose in the session but promised that it would "push the envelope."

"I think we can get it done in about a day and the Democrats, if you think they hate me now . . . Wow," LePage told the gathering.

LePage ended up shelving his idea for a special session after his remarks about a secret plan caused a swarm of media attention and accusations of political game-playing by his opponents. When the secret policy was finally revealed through leaks from his office, it didn't quite live up to the hype and didn't seem to fit the criteria he had described. The plan was to renegotiate the state's liquor contract and use the money to pay back the remaining hospital debt–a significant piece of public policy, but not a particularly contentious or ideologically divisive idea.

When the new legislature convened, however, LePage showed just how quickly he could turn a policy landscape on which there was bipartisan agreement into a divided political battlefield. He began to insist that his specific payback plan be considered outside the normal budgeting process (through which legislators might have found other uses for the liquor revenue or other ways to pay back the hospitals) and began to take political hostages to make sure he got his way. He first announced that he would refuse to issue the bonds approved by voters at the last election until his hospital plan was approved, and then declared that he would begin vetoing any bill that was not his hospital debt legislation.

LePage didn't completely stick to these threats, allowing some bills to become law without his signature, but he certainly succeeded in ramping up the pressure. He continued to escalate the situation with a constant drumbeat of public statements about Democrats refusing to pay the state's debts.

In April 2013 he was joined by his personal pressure group, Maine People Before Politics. The organization, headed by his senior campaign adviser, began running TV ads promoting his plan and attacking former Governor Baldacci (who at that point was seen as a potential 2014 challenger to LePage) for not having settled the debt.

Democrats were caught flat-footed. They agreed that the hospitals should be paid but weren't sure LePage's proposal was the right way to do it, preferring instead to examine a wider range of policy options within the context of the looming budget gap. This position didn't work well as a public message, however, or as a sound-bite response to LePage's accusations that they were immorally reneging on the state's obligations.

Eventually, Democratic leaders attempted their own political maneuver, combining LePage's hospital debt payment plan with their own bill to accept federal funds to expand health care coverage and insisting that they be passed as a package. They quickly proved that they didn't have the stomach for the fight, however, and in their first press conference announcing the compromise they refused to rule out passing LePage's plan as a separate bill. LePage sensed weakness, vetoed the package, and, without a hint of irony, used the incident to accuse Democrats of playing politics. Legislative Republicans upheld his veto.

In the end, LePage got exactly what he wanted. His repayment plan was unanimously approved in the house and senate, the Medicaid expansion was left out of the deal, and he successfully turned what might have been a bipartisan policy agreement into a bruising partisan victory. Even after the issue was decided, he continued to claim that he was the only one who had been in favor of paying the hospitals and that Democrats had been against paying the state's debts. In the fall of 2013 he took a victory lap of Maine's hospitals, holding press conferences to deliver giant checks bearing his signature.

The policy outcome was also a win for LePage's Health and Human Services commissioner, Mary Mayhew, who had previously served as head lobbyist for the Maine Hospital Association.

The entire incident hearkened back to the "Front Page LePage" tactics that candidate LePage had bragged were a big part of his success as mayor of Waterville, but that he had mostly been unable to replicate as governor. LePage crafted a simple message, used every square inch of his bully pulpit to proclaim it loudly to the media, drowned out his opponents, and got his way.

Because the two issues became intertwined and because the debate was so divisive, the conflict over hospital repayment may have hurt the chances of the legislature reaching the two-thirds agreement needed to overrule LePage and accept federal funding for MaineCare, even though the coverage expansion, if passed, would provide a great deal more long-term funding for Maine's hospitals than the liquor contract deal.

Medicaid expansion may never have had a real chance. In addition to opposition by LePage and key Republican allies in the legislature, the acceptance of federal funds was specifically targeted for defeat by the same powerful coalition of national conservative groups, activists, and donors that has been behind much of LePage's agenda.

One key to LePage's success on this issue was the return of a figure from the fight over insurance reforms, Tarren Bragdon. After successfully shepherding the rate hike bill through the legislature, Bragdon had decamped from the Maine Heritage Policy Center to a new, nationally focused organization he founded in Naples, Florida, called the Foundation for Government Accountability (FGA). The FGA has deep ties to national organizations like the American Leadership Exchange Council (ALEC), the State Policy Network (SPN), and Americans for Prosperity (AFP), all groups founded or funded by libertarian billionaire oil magnates Charles and David Koch. The Kochs and their allies have helped to build most of the infrastructure of the American far right and have poured hundreds of millions of dollars into conservative causes such as stopping health care reform and denying the existence of global climate change.

FGA doesn't release information about its donors, but some hints about their financing have made it into the public domain. In 2012 (the last year for which records are available), tax documents filed by other organizations indicate that FGA received $213,500 from Donors Trust, a foundation created to allow conservative donors, including the Koch brothers, to give anonymously to various causes. FGA received $108,150 from SPN, an ALEC-founded and Koch-funded umbrella group for state-level conservative organizations, of which both FGA and MHPC are affiliates. The group also received $25,000 from the Atlas Economic Research Foundation, another group with close ties to the Kochs.

FGA has advocated against health care expansion in a number of states, and FGA Senior Fellow Christie Herrera has crisscrossed the country for speaking engagements and to give legislative testimony against the expansion bills. Before joining the newly formed FGA, Herrera was director of ALEC's Health and Human Services Task Force, and she still maintains a hand in the inner workings of the corporate-controlled policy incubator. A cache of documents obtained as a result of an open records lawsuit by the Center for Media and Democracy shows that Herrera, from her post at FGA, wrote the anti-Medicaid expansion resolution that ALEC adopted in 2013. E-mails from Herrera show that she convinced three state legislators in different states to introduce her motion as their own and wrote introductory remarks and talking points for them to use at ALEC's 2013 Spring Task Force Summit.

FGA and Bragdon took a leading role in shoring up support for LePage's goal of refusing the federal health care funding in Maine. The result was a remarkably cynical campaign involving the denial of political and policy reality and so much spin and doublespeak that the *Bangor Daily News* editorial page termed it "straight out of *1984.*"

Among other activities, FGA and their partners at Americans for Prosperity released the results of a poll that used biased questions and outright lies (for instance, claiming that one-third of those eligible for expanded coverage were "former prison inmates"–a near impossibility given Maine's lowest-in-the-nation incarceration rate) in order to claim that a plurality of Mainers oppose expansion.

FGA may also have had a hand in one of the most controversial initiatives of the LePage administration, a no-bid contract giving conservative activist Gary Alexander almost a million dollars to review Maine's public assistance programs and write what was termed a "Medicaid expansion feasibility study."

Alexander has close ties to FGA, having worked with the organization several times during and following his rocky tenure as secretary of Pennsylvania's Department of Public Welfare.

In 2013, Alexander joined Herrera for a public conference call on health care policy with FGA supporters.

"I thank you, Christie, and your great organization for organizing this," said Alexander as they ended the call. "You guys are a tremendous repository for all of this information and I look forward to continuing to work with you as we solve the country's most vexing problems."

Alexander got his chance to continue that partnership when the LePage administration hired his consultancy to perform its welfare review. Sam Adolphson, a former policy analyst at MHPC under Bragdon and now a Maine Department of Health and Human Services employee, was named program administrator for the study.

Alexander delivered exactly what the LePage administration needed: a report that conflicted with the results of every independent examination of the issue, which had found clear economic and health care benefits from MaineCare expansion. The report appeared to show that accepting the funds would actually result in a significant cost to the state. To reach this conclusion, Alexander ignored the broader economic impact of the federal funds and made strange assumptions such as that the state poverty rate would increase by more than 30 percent over the next ten years. A subsequent review of Alexander's work by national experts, commissioned by the American Association of Retired Persons, revealed that the report also contained a $575 million multiplication error.

The *Portland Press Herald* called the report "shoddy" and "riddled with errors and ridiculous assumptions." The *Bangor Daily News* deemed it a failure and "a political document disguised as impartial analysis created at taxpayers' expense."

In contrast, an independent study by the nonpartisan Kaiser Foundation found that accepting federal funds would save Maine $690 million over ten years, above and beyond the costs of the increased coverage. Another study, conducted by researchers at Harvard and City University of New York, found that, by one measurement, 157 lives could be saved in the first year alone by accepting funds and expanding coverage.

Despite its transparent flaws, the political and policy dog-and-pony show put on by LePage and his national allies was enough to keep key Republican legislators in line. A few GOP senators and representatives joined Democrats in advancing a series of compromise proposals to accept the health care funding, but all were rejected by LePage and fell just a few votes short of the two-thirds support necessary to override his vetoes.

As with many of LePage's policies, an irony of the MaineCare expansion debate is that many of LePage's strongest supporters–Tea Party members who reside in rural areas and live just above the poverty line–are among those who would benefit most from the expansion.

In fact, many those who would be most affected by the expansion seem to fit the perfect stereotype of traditional self-sufficiency that LePage and Tea Party supporters claim to be fighting to preserve.

Richard Holt is one example. He's a commercial fisherman in South Portland who has held a lobster license since 1974. A Republican, Holt and his family have supported the GOP for generations. He believes so deeply in the party's values of responsibility and independence that when he built his boat with his own hands, he refused to take a state tax break on the materials, considering it to be too much like a handout.

When it comes to health care, however, Holt has no options. An injury he suffered in his twenties has become chronic and has limited how much he's able to fish and his ability to make a living. There are no affordable private insurance options for someone with his income and occupation. What has allowed him to keep working at all is the medicine and care he's been able to access through MaineCare, but he lost it at the beginning of 2014 with the implementation of LePage's cuts.

For Holt, the result of LePage's rejection of federal funding will not be increased independence and more of an incentive to work. Without care, he'll likely lose his livelihood and his house, which has been in his family for generations.

Tom Benne is another fiercely independent Mainer whose self-sufficiency and work ethic even the most hard-core Tea Party believer would have to admire. He and his wife own a small farm in Whitefield where they grow their own food and raise some cattle. When he isn't farming, Benne works for his neighbors doing construction and fixing cars and tractors.

Benne has had arthritis since he was eighteen, and in recent years it has become acutely severe. Things got so bad that by noon each day he could no longer walk. Because he had MaineCare coverage, he was able to have surgery that let him walk again and get back to work. It also may have saved his wife's life. According to Benne, the only reason they went to the hospital when she began experiencing symptoms of a heart attack is because they knew they had coverage.

Holt and Benne are concrete examples of how LePage's ideological stance against accepting money from the Affordable Care Act will affect individual Mainers and take them out of the workforce. The broader consequences for the state are just as dire. The Harvard/CUNY study found that in 2014, 3,137 more Mainers will suffer from clinical depression and 953 more Mainers will face catastrophic medical expenditures as a result of Maine's rejection of federal funds. The Maine Center for Economic Policy predicts that rejecting the funding will cost the state 4,400 new jobs, many of them high-paying health care positions in rural areas.

The consequences of LePage's rigid Tea Party ideology have likely been manifested more immediately and visibly in health care than in any other policy area. His decision to stick with the Tea Party and ALEC position against Obamacare, even in the face of mountains of evidence of the cost to Maine's people and the economy, has directly resulted in human suffering and loss of life.

Other actions by the LePage administration on health care have had less drastic consequences but fit a similar pattern. One high-profile administrative decision taken by LePage's DHHS was to privatize the MaineCare ride program. When LePage became governor, the provision of rides to medical appointments for patients with transportation difficulties was handled by a constellation of small, local nonprofits across the state. In 2013, however, the LePage administration replaced that system with a broker model under which two for-profit, out-of-state companies took over ride scheduling and logistics. Coordinated Transportation Systems (CTS), based in Connecticut, was given a $28.3 million contract to handle rides for most of the state, and Atlanta-based LogistiCare won a $5.1 million contract to handle rides in York County in southern Maine.

LogistiCare had previously given an undisclosed amount of money to the LePage transition/Maine People Before Politics and was awarded the contract despite a history of complaints and controversy about their management of rides programs in other states. A month after its contract began in 2013, the company gave the maximum allowable contribution to LePage's reelection campaign.

The results of the change were immediately disastrous for Mainers needing rides. Calls went unanswered, pick-ups were cancelled, or drivers never showed, forcing sick and injured patients across the state to miss appointments and wait hours for rides that never came.

Complaints flooded in. Maine's newspapers ran a long series of articles detailing the problems, and the Democratic legislature began holding hearings. One particularly dramatic moment came when executives from CTS and LogistiCare testified before a legislative committee that they had fixed most of the issues. In response, Representative Matthew Peterson pulled out his cell phone and called the number patients were meant to dial to arrange a ride through CTS. He held the phone to his microphone as an automated voice said, "I'm sorry for any inconvenience. Goodbye," and the line went dead.

The problems slowly improved, but complaints continued to trickle in about missed rides and drivers choosing routes and patients based on where they could get the highest reimbursements. The legislature passed a bill to cancel the contracts and return to the previous, cheaper, more efficient nonprofit model, but LePage vetoed the legislation.

Finally acknowledging the scale of the problem, in January 2014 the LePage administration announced that they would not be renewing the contract with CTS. Rather than return to the old system, however, they announced that LogistiCare would be taking over in most of the state.

The human and economic costs of the ride program privatization will likely be far less than those from LePage's refusal of federal health care funding or even the insurance rate hikes, but the issue fits the same pattern seen throughout LePage's tenure. His actions on health care support a corporate-backed ideological agenda at the expense of the health and well-being of Mainers.

chapter 11 Public Assistance

I n his campaign speeches in 2010, one of Governor LePage's most-repeated anecdotes was about an employee of his at Marden's Surplus and Salvage who was struggling to make ends meet.

Sometimes LePage said the anonymous employee, a single mother, was making $10 an hour. At other times he said she made $12.50, but her problem was always that she could be making more (either by accepting a small raise or by working an hour more per week) but didn't because she feared her family would lose access to government programs including heating assistance and food stamps.

LePage's answer to this problem on the stump was downright compassionate. He promised that as governor he wouldn't just cut welfare in the hopes that it would force the woman to work more, but would instead increase assistance overall and reduce it more gradually if and when people's incomes improved, in order to provide a series of steps all the way up to a living wage.

Outlining his proposal at a Tea Party rally in January 2010, LePage said, "What we need to really do is to stage it. I want to have a five-tier system. The system starts at the poverty level and it goes to the earning wage. We have five tiers, every time you reach a tier, instead of taking you off welfare completely, we take 20 percent of your benefits away, let you keep 80 percent, then when you reach the next tier, the same thing, so once you've gone through your five tiers you're at a living wage and you don't need welfare. It's not an automatic cut the minute you make an extra dollar."

Public assistance programs such as Temporary Assistance for Needy Families (TANF) are already tiered to some degree, but

LePage's proposed innovation was to make those tiers more defined and to raise the maximum income level at which Mainers would still be eligible for some assistance to a living wage. In 2010, in order to meet the official definition of a living wage in Maine as calculated by the Maine Department of Labor, a single parent with one child would have had to work full-time and make $18.21 an hour. Organizations such as the Maine Center for Economic Policy and the national Alliance for a Just Society, using slightly different models of the costs of living in Maine, have calculated a living wage to be slightly higher.

Unlike many of LePage's proposals, this one, had he attempted to implement it once in office, would likely have found widespread bipartisan support.

"We certainly would have supported that. It would have given people exactly the help they need to survive in this economy, keep their families together, and find work," explained Christine Hastedt, public policy director for Maine Equal Justice Partners, an organization that assists Mainers in poverty and advocates on their behalf. "Right now the combination of wages and the support most people who need this assistance receive brings them nowhere near a living wage."

LePage also called for new outreach to and health care for the mentally ill as a way of reducing the need for public assistance and for incarceration.

"The other thing that we need to do in general assistance is right now our jails are packed with people with mental illness. We've abandoned our people who are ill and we have to stop that. We have to get these people proper doctors so they can get their medication," said LePage. "We keep them on medication, if they don't want to stay on medication then we go to the next step, but once they're medicated we work with them to live an independent life and get back into society with jobs."

Much of the rest of LePage's rhetoric around public assistance was the kind of anti-welfare messaging common among Tea Party politicians (he called assistance programs "the shackles of economic slavery," among other things), and some of his other proposals on the subject weren't anywhere near as compassionate, such as a strict five-year time limit for assistance programs. ("At the end of five years, if you still require general assistance, I will personally pay for a bus ticket to Massachusetts," he said.) But some of the policy proposals he discussed the most during his campaign were humane, progressive, and likely to improve the lives of people in poverty.

During his inauguration address in 2011, LePage reiterated his belief in the need for a tiered system, although he didn't mention the number of tiers or the target of a living wage. As an example of the kind of people his desired system would help, LePage referred to Jennifer Cloukey, a single mother of four from Bowdoinham who relied on TANF and the Supplemental Nutritional Assistance Program (SNAP) as she completed a degree in nursing. He said that he hoped her experience of accessing the programs on a temporary basis while working or building skills to succeed in the workforce would soon be the norm. Cloukey, a LePage supporter, sat in the front row for his speech and gave media interviews afterward.

Advocates for the needy argued that Cloukey's family was already typical of those receiving assistance. A survey of 1,000 of the 14,000 Maine families receiving assistance through TANF in 2010, conducted by professors at the University of Maine and the University of New England, found that families accessed welfare assistance for a median of 1.5 years. Of those who received benefits for more than the five-year maximum proposed by LePage, 88 percent either had disabilities that made it difficult to work or were caring for children with disabilities.

Once he was in office, however, LePage stopped talking about compassionate, tiered welfare programs and instead focused on new restrictions and cuts. He also increased investigation and prosecution of fraud and trumpeted cases of abuse. Based on the amount of legislative effort and the number of public statements made on the subject, one might easily forget that TANF, the system providing the cash payments that most people think of when they think of welfare, makes up less than 1 percent of the state budget.

LePage's first budget contained several proposals to restrict access to TANF, including a ban on legal non-citizen immigrants using the program for the first five years of their residency in Maine, a five-year maximum for all TANF recipients, and new regulations that would strip benefits from children if their parents failed to fulfill work search requirements. (Previously only the parents' benefits were lost.)

A provision that allowed drug testing of welfare recipients was also passed but never put into practice due to concerns about the cost and constitutionality of the measure. A similar law was in operation for four months in Florida before a federal judge issued an injunction halting the practice. During that time, the program cost far more in enforcement than it saved in reduced payments to welfare recipients.

The restrictions have had a significant impact on Maine's public assistance programs. In September 2013, Governor LePage bragged about the effects in a statewide radio address.

"Recent data shows that the Temporary Assistance for Needy Families program caseload has decreased from about 15,000 cases in January 2011 to about 9,000 cases in June of this year. This reflects a decrease in caseload of 41 percent," said LePage. "We are experiencing a drop in welfare assistance by promoting job preparation and work."

Despite LePage's claims, however, there is no evidence that the changes have led to more Mainers on TANF finding work.

In part, the drop in TANF enrollment can be ascribed to a slowly improving national economy. The 15,000 families who received assistance in 2011 represented the peak of an increase from the roughly 12,000 who used TANF in 2007, prior to the economic collapse and recession. By June 2012, prior to the implementation of the five-year restriction, the TANF caseload stood at 13,302 families.

To date, there is no published study of how many non-citizen immigrants denied TANF assistance have found employment since the implementation of the new restrictions. From 2012 to 2013, however, Professor Sandra Butler at the University of Maine conducted a thorough examination of the preliminary effects of the new five-year limit on assistance. She found that during the implementation phase between June and October 2012, more than 1,500 families, including an estimated 2,700 children, lost access to help through TANF.

As was predicted based on the high percentage of individuals with disabilities in this population, very few of those stripped of TANF support were able to find additional employment after their assistance was cut. In fact, Butler's study found no statistically significant increase in employment.

What Butler did find is that a group of families who were already beset with the effects of deep and lasting poverty were plunged into a new level of deprivation in the few months since they lost access to public assistance. Of those who lost access to TANF, 68.5 percent were relying on food banks for nutrition, 35 percent had their utilities shut off, and 15 percent had already been evicted from their homes.

Butler's findings are based on a survey of and personal interviews with these struggling Mainers. One of those impacted by the new restriction on TANF assistance was Sarah, a single mother in her twenties with two children and a GED. Despite not having a vehicle, Sarah had been taking advantage of childcare assistance through TANF to pursue a degree as a medical assistant, while also conducting an extensive search for a stopgap job to help her family scrape by.

"I've gone to every place that is in a reasonable distance from where I am and filled out applications more than once in all these places and called them 50 million times," Sarah told the interviewer. "I've gone to all the McDonalds; I've gone to all the Burger Kings; I've gone to all the Dunkin Donuts, Sam's, the Big Apples, the Rite Aids."

Sarah and her family were pursuing exactly the path out of poverty that LePage had lauded, and her story bears a striking resemblance to the example of Jennifer Cloukey cited in his inaugural address. Sarah's story has a very different ending from Cloukey's, however, thanks to LePage's reforms. When she lost her childcare support through TANF, Sarah was forced to drop out of college. In addition to having no degree and no job prospects, even at minimum wage, she was then saddled with a year's worth of student loans for an education she suddenly couldn't afford to complete. Her electricity and phone service were cut off, and she was forced to rely on the local food bank to feed her family. At the time of her interview, she didn't see any options for a way out.

Sarah's experience is exactly the opposite of how candidate LePage said things would work during his administration. Instead of programs to help struggling families find a way out of poverty and five new tiers to lift them up as they found new opportunities, the lifelines these families depended on were cut. According to Butler's study, more people became homeless than found jobs thanks to LePage's public assistance reforms.

With LePage's cuts, much of the burden of helping families facing hard times fell to towns and cities in Maine through a program called General Assistance, which provides financial and other assistance for families experiencing hardship. Even these resources were made scarcer, however, by LePage's insistence that Maine municipalities cut back their budgets and his across-the-board cuts to state revenue-sharing with towns, further limiting their options.

Almost as large as the gap between LePage's welfare rhetoric and the effects of his actual policies is the distance between his continued public statements on the issue and reality.

At the Concerned Women's Network event in October 2013, LePage declared that "about 47 percent of able-bodied people in the state of Maine don't work." The comment made national news, both because of the ridiculousness of the figure and its similarity to the well-known, secretly recorded remarks made by Republican presidential candidate Mitt Romney during his 2012 campaign, in which he alleged that 47 percent of Americans pay no income tax and "are dependent upon government."

Politifact, a well-regarded national organization staffed by professional journalists and dedicated to fact-checking political statements, gave LePage's statement a "Pants on Fire" rating for what they said was a "ridiculous claim." The real number of Maine residents who can work and don't is closer to 1 percent.

LePage sounded a similar note during his State of the State address in 2012 when he strayed from his prepared remarks in order to deliver a special message to a particular constituency. "Get off the couch and get yourself a job!" he told the unemployed.

In addition to lobbing insults and fabricating numbers to serve his arguments about public assistance, one of LePage's favorite rhetorical tactics is to link spending for cash assistance for the poor, what most people consider welfare, with health care coverage and other government programs that include some form of means testing, usually MaineCare. This serves to inflate the number of people served by and dollars spent on what he considers a bloated welfare system.

In a September 2013 radio address, LePage used anti-welfare language to argue that the state shouldn't accept the federal funding to expand health care coverage for the working poor. "Liberal politicians now want to expand welfare again and add 70,000 people to the MaineCare program," said LePage. "They keep telling Mainers that this expansion would be free because the federal government would pay for it. But folks, as I keep saying, there is no free lunch."

Sometimes, however, LePage's message discipline in this area breaks down.

"One thing you should think of is breaking welfare out of Medicaid–that's a big one," said LePage at the Informed Women's Network event just a month after his on-air statement that Medicaid and welfare were one and the same. "We need to separate it–and many states have done it and it works. You separate welfare from health care."

LePage was referring to breaking apart the streamlined, computerized system that allows Maine people to learn what means-tested state programs they may be eligible for, instead forcing Mainers to fill out different forms for TANF, SNAP, and MaineCare. The combined system was implemented in the early 2000s and has significantly increased efficiency and decreased administrative costs for the Maine Department of Health and Human Services, which oversees the various programs. Breaking the applications apart wouldn't do anything to address people's actual needs, only make it more difficult and frustrating for them to access assistance.

This idea of denying access through bureaucratic attrition is a common theme in LePage's welfare reforms, and a stark departure from his campaign promises to eliminate red tape wherever he found it. The changes he has implemented seem designed not to help struggling families or even reduce costs to the state (his anti-fraud programs, for instance, have so far cost far more than they have recovered), but rather to punish those who have had the temerity to fall on hard times.

Despite a slowly improving national economy, the Department of Housing and Urban Development estimates that homelessness in Maine has increased by 26.8 percent since the implementation of LePage's changes to public assistance programs.

In 2014, LePage launched a new legislative assault on public assistance programs, proposing a new raft of cuts and restrictions. Most were rejected by the Democratic majorities. He also continued to rhetorically link health care to welfare in every public statement during the debate over accepting federal funding to expand Maine-Care coverage.

The governor and his advisors see the specter of welfare fraud and the othering of those who receive public assistance as a potent tool to help motivate their Tea Party base and make sure they make it to the polls in November. Demonizing those he sees as the "lazy poor" will likely continue to be a key part of his reelection campaign.

chapter 12 Labor

overnor LePage likes to have an enemy. According to members of his staff, having an opponent animates him in a way few other things do. In policy debates, LePage often frames an issue as a battle between two polarized sides, with himself, of course, on the side of justice, common sense, and the average Mainer. Even when Republicans controlled the legislature and he had his way more often than not, LePage often portrayed himself as an underdog, fighting an uphill battle against what he has called the "country club" establishment and the entrenched interests in Augusta.

One of LePage's favorite enemies is organized labor, especially unions representing public employees. The rhetoric he has leveled against "union bosses" and "corrupt" state employees has been caustic, and his tone has been matched by his administration's policy of rolling back workplace protections and attempting to undermine collective bargaining rights. From cutting pensions to promoting so-called "right to work" legislation and directly inserting himself into the state's unemployment claims and appeals process, LePage has done his best to change Maine's labor landscape to give more power to employers and less to their employees.

On several occasions, LePage has compared himself with Scott Walker, the controversial Wisconsin governor who sparked a months-long protest in and around the State House in Madison as he pushed through anti-union legislation. LePage seems to relish the idea of a similar high-profile confrontation in Maine.

"Quite frankly, once they start reading our budget they're going to leave Wisconsin and come to Maine, because we're going after 'right to work,'" LePage told *Politico* shortly after taking office.

It's ironic, then, that LePage's biggest public fight and perhaps his most lasting legacy on labor issues might be a symbolic spat over a piece of public art.

On March 22, 2011, LePage's acting Department of Labor commissioner sent an e-mail to staff stating that "we have received feedback that the administration building is not perceived as equally receptive to both businesses and workers–primarily because of the nature of the mural in the lobby and the names of our conference rooms." The commissioner announced that she would be seeking a new home for the mural and holding a "renaming contest" to solicit new monikers for the conference rooms, one of which was named after Frances Perkins, a Mainer who helped to implement the New Deal as President Franklin Roosevelt's secretary of labor and was the first woman to lead a federal department.

The mural is a large installation of eleven panels that depict workers in traditional Maine industries and significant events in the state's labor history. When asked by the media, LePage said he had received an anonymous fax complaining that the artwork, then displayed in the department's lobby, was creating an unwelcoming atmosphere for business owners and representatives who visited the building. Acting on this tip, he had the artwork removed and stored in a location that he refused to reveal.

The removal was quickly noticed and sparked a backlash from artists and labor activists as well as a frenzy of attention from state and national media.

Before the controversy ended two years later and the mural was safely transferred to the Maine State Museum, protests would be held, a lawsuit would be filed and defended against by the attorney general, the U.S. Department of Labor would weigh in and ask for their money back (the artwork had been purchased with a combination of state and federal funds), a reporter would file a freedom of access request for security camera footage in an attempt to find out where the mural had been stashed, and a particularly creative group of activists would use a powerful projector to stage a nighttime display of giant versions of panels of the mural on the exterior of the State House.

Governor LePage made a number of colorful and conflicting statements about the affair that helped to prod the story along, at one point calling those who opposed the removal "idiots" and suggesting they "get over themselves." A search of Lexis/Nexis's news database returns more than 700 results with the terms "LePage" and "mural." The controversy was mentioned eight times in the pages of the *New York Times* alone.

That may seem like a lot of effort and ink spilled for what, in the scheme of things, wasn't a particularly important government action, but the mural served as a symbolic focal point for LePage and his labor opponents. Government budgetary policy and workers' rights laws can be complex issues, but the mural fight was easy to conceptualize and became a handy stand-in for the larger conflict.

The debate over the LePage administration's role in labor and workers' rights issues began even before LePage took office. LePage did not include a labor representative on his transition advisory committees, and in December 2010 an e-mail sent by incoming LePage communications and legislative affairs director Dan Demeritt to fellow Republicans (and subsequently leaked to progressive blogger Gerald Weinand) raised fears that the new governor was planning to politicize the state workforce. In the letter, which contained the subject line "incumbent protection," Demeritt outlined ways in which Republicans could take political advantage of their newly won incumbency and control of government (including a prescient description of the "big symbolic check" hospital-debt press conferences that LePage would hold almost three years later).

"Once we take office, Paul will put 11,000 bureaucrats to work getting Republicans reelected," promised Demeritt in the letter, a statement many took to mean that LePage would be pressuring state employees to take actions to politically benefit Republicans.

Demeritt said it was simply a poor choice of words, but words matter, as was shown a few weeks later when Republicans attempted to eliminate the legislature's Labor Committee, merging its functions and issue portfolio with the Business, Research and Economic Development Committee. Democratic and Republican leaders eventually compromised on a plan that allowed the merger to proceed but added the word "labor" to the beginning of the merged committee's name as a way of ensuring that labor issues would still be given a high priority.

Once the new legislature had solved the issue of committee nomenclature, it turned its attention to more pressing matters, such as LePage's plan to cut the pensions of 75,000 current and former teachers and state employees. Much like Maine's obligations to hospitals, the state pension system had been underfunded for years as the state government had put off making payments and the stock market had dipped.

LePage claimed a moral imperative to repay the hospital debt, but the debt to teachers and state employees incited no such compunction. Instead, he proposed that teachers and state employees pay for the deficit themselves by increasing their contributions to the pension system from 7.65 percent of their salaries to 9.65 percent.

At the same time, state payments to the pension fund would be decreased from 5.5 percent of teacher and state employee salaries to 3.5 percent. Even before this proposed 2 percent reduction, the state's contribution to the pension fund was less than the 6.2 percent state contribution that would be required if these same employees were enrolled in Social Security instead. Because of their pensions, Maine's teachers and state employees aren't eligible to accrue Social Security credits while employed with the state.

"I know some teachers and retirees are struggling, but we need honest and shared solutions to solve our pension problem," said LePage while pushing for the changes.

When John McKernan, Maine's last Republican governor before LePage, had proposed cuts to state workers' salaries as part of his 1990 budget plan, he had also voluntarily given back some of his own salary as a gesture of solidarity. LePage did not follow his predecessor's example. Because his salary and benefits were governed by a different statute and protected from immediate modification by the state constitution, instead of sharing his part of what he said was a "shared solution," LePage's plan would have made him the only employee of the executive branch whose pension remained untouched.

"We don't spend a lot of time trying to cover a political angle," said Demeritt, the author of that memo about making sure they covered every political angle, in explaining the lack of shared sacrifice by LePage.

The budget that was eventually passed approached the pension debt in a slightly different way than LePage had proposed, by cutting back on retirees' cost of living increases rather than making cuts up front. The burden of the changes, however, remained squarely on the backs of teachers and state employees.

The LePage administration made no secret of what they planned to do with the money they saved.

"The pension savings in this budget allows for taxes to be cut by $203 million over the biennium," said LePage budget director Sawin Millett in testimony before the Appropriations and Financial Affairs Committee, referring to LePage's planned income and estate tax cuts that predominantly benefited the wealthy. It was a clear statement of the priorities of the new administration.

The other fight LePage picked on labor issues during his first year in office didn't go quite as well for his administration. Although LePage imagined that his attack on collective bargaining would rally supporters to his side just as Scott Walker had attracted supporters in Wisconsin, the response to the "right to work" bills backed by the LePage administration was much more muted.

The most high-profile legislation on the issue, submitted by Republican Representative Tom Winsor and meant to undercut the financial base of the Maine State Employees Union, would have allowed public employees to opt out of paying union dues even though the union would still be responsible for representing them in collective bargaining and workplace disputes. Consideration of the bill was delayed by the Republican leadership as they struggled to hold their caucus together on the issue. After intense lobbying by unions and progressive groups, the bill was first carried over to the second session of the legislature in 2012 and then left to die at the committee level without ever getting a vote. A similar bill targeting private-sector unions was "indefinitely postponed" by a vote of the house of representatives.

LePage has continued to rail against unions, attempting to resurrect similar anti-union legislation in 2013 and again in early 2014. His attempts again failed, predictably facing an even tougher reaction than they had under a Republican-controlled legislature in previous years. Despite his best efforts to keep the conflict alive, LePage has never been able to gain the same kind of legislative traction and national attention as Governor Walker.

chapter 13 Jobs

One of the most memorable lines of LePage's stump speech during his 2010 campaign was a promise to destroy and replace a sign at Maine's border with New Hampshire. "If I win, the first thing I'm doing is I'm going to Kittery and there's a great big sign that says 'Maine: Vacationland,'" Lepage told a Tea Party gathering in Augusta in November 2009. "Well I'm gonna chop 'er down and we're going to put a new one up and it's going to say 'Maine: Open for Business.'"

With the help of his Tea Party supporters, LePage did put up his "Open for Business" sign, right below the iconic blue "Welcome to Maine: The Way Life Should Be" placard next to Interstate 95 at the border with New Hampshire. Ironically, the new sign was manufactured in Alabama. A few months later, the sign disappeared and was presumed to have been stolen. The Maine Aggregate Association, a lobby organization for a group of sand and gravel businesses, later purchased a replacement.

The sign was meant as a symbol of the attitude LePage wanted to instill in the State of Maine, a change in perspective that he said was key to his plans to create jobs. On the campaign trail, he was fond of saying that the only jobs government can create are government jobs (which he opposed on principle) and that the best thing government can do to encourage private-sector job growth is to create a business-friendly environment and then get out of the way. This philosophy underpinned many of LePage's policy priorities and was invoked to justify the rollback of environmental regulations, tax cuts for the wealthy, his attempts to weaken unions and collective bargaining, and his push for less restrictive child labor laws.

Early in his term, LePage held "Red Tape Workshops" across the state, where he heard from local business owners about regulations that impacted their ability to grow their businesses and create jobs. The tour culminated in a raft of regulatory changes proposed to the legislature, many of them focused on decreasing environmental protections. It was later revealed that a majority of the proposals had come not from the workshops, but from lobbyists mostly representing large corporations.

LePage also created "Account Executive" positions within the Department of Economic and Community Development (DECD) and new online tools meant to help businesses navigate state permitting and regulatory processes quickly and easily.

In many areas, however, LePage's laissez-faire philosophy has led him to ignore opportunities for state government to have a positive impact on job creation. At other times, he has made decisions, based either on Tea Party ideology or his own confrontational style, that have significantly harmed Maine's job market and economy. As much as he claimed to want to create a new, positive state attitude toward job creation, his own negative attitude toward the state and his prioritization of politics over shared prosperity have resulted in one of the worst job records of any governor in the country.

One of the first and most obviously harmful decisions was the appointment of Philip Congdon to be DECD commissioner. LePage corrected that mistake when he fired the inexperienced Tea Party ideologue following his series of offensive remarks (see Chapter 5), but other, similar actions have had a more lasting impact.

Small businesses are the engine of Maine's economy. According to the Small Business Administration, they make up 97.2 percent of all employers in the state and account for 59.7 percent of all private-sector jobs. The LePage administration, however, has often prioritized the needs of large, out-of-state corporate interests ahead of local entrepreneurs. A prime example is the Republican health insurance legislation passed in 2011 (see Chapter 10). These so-called reforms reduced regulations and made ideological sense for LePage to support, but the real effect was allowing large insurance companies to charge far more for individual and small business plans. Small businesses across the state saw their health insurance costs, one of the major expenses of running a business, increase by double- and triple-digit percentages. The effects were felt most acutely in rural Maine, where the economic climate was already more harsh.

One of the ways that state government can most directly influence the job market and local economy is through infrastructure spending. In Maine and other states, this kind of investment is often paid for by issuing infrastructure bonds. This state borrowing leverages federal funds and improves the economic prospects of the state while also creating short-term employment.

LePage's position on bonding has varied widely during his tenure in office. At times he has railed against any and all government debt and sought to limit the amount the state could borrow. At other times he has championed, at least rhetorically, infrastructure bonds as a way to create jobs and improve transportation links that are important to commerce. Almost invariably, however, LePage has used the bonds and the jobs they represent as a tool to advance his ideological agenda, often at the cost of Maine's economy.

Maine voters approved $40 million in bonds by referendum in 2010 and another $64 million in 2012, but LePage refused to allow the money to be borrowed (a technical requirement that no previous governor had exploited). He then held the spending hostage in an attempt to influence one political fight after another–first saying he would hold the bonds until legislators approved his hospital repayment plan, then conditioning the bonds on approval of his budget, and later threatening not to release them until legislators agreed to his plan to cut municipal revenue sharing.

Holding the bonds was one of a number of similar tactics–including threatening to veto all bills that came across his desk and refusing to submit a supplemental budget–that LePage used to turn the normal mechanisms of his office into tools of political warfare.

LePage's politicization of the bonding process also extended to the local level. Some of the money was slated to go to local community development, including projects that were already underway in towns across Maine. In order to allow some of these job-creating projects to go forward, in 2012, a few months before the legislative elections, LePage wrote a series of letters guaranteeing that state money would eventually be available, in essence offering a guarantee for local debt.

There was a specific pattern to the letters, however. Of the eleven towns with planned development projects, LePage initially wrote letters only for five. Every one of the five was represented by Republicans in both the houses of the state legislature. None of the four towns with Democratic representatives received similar assistance from the governor.

Perhaps the greatest example of LePage's politics and ideology slowing growth is his refusal to accept federal health care funds for MaineCare expansion. In a state the size of Maine, the 4,400 jobs the expansion would create would mean a significant improvement in the local economy. The health care expansion would also allow coverage for many current small business owners going without and would allow others to be entrepreneurial for the first time without worrying about a lack of coverage.

Other LePage actions affecting investment and job creation in the state range from his interference in the StatOil deal (see Chapter 7) to his frequent and false denigrations of the intelligence and preparedness of Maine graduates (Chapter 8) or of the work ethic of Maine people.

LePage and his supporters have argued that, overall, his economic improvement efforts, regulatory changes, and focus on shifting general attitudes toward business have been successful, and they point to an unemployment rate that has steadily decreased over his term, but these claims are deeply misleading.

The employment rate doesn't tell the whole story. While unemployment is falling across the country as the United States continues its long, slow recovery from the 2008 crash and the subsequent economic recession, Maine is recovering much more slowly and has fallen behind other states economically during LePage's tenure. Compared with the rest of the country and especially the rest of New England, job growth in the state has been anemic.

State and federal labor statistics show that from January 2011, when LePage took office, through March 2014, Maine ranked forty-ninth in the country in total job growth, regaining jobs lost in the recession at a slower rate than all but one other state. Maine had recovered only 49 percent of lost jobs by the end of that period, compared with 93 percent nationally and 96 percent in New England. By May 2014, when employment nationally finally surpassed its pre-recession peak–with 8.8 million more people working than in the February 2010 trough–Maine had still regained only about half of its 30,000 lost jobs.

Despite LePage's claim that 47 percent of Mainers are shirking employment, the problem isn't a lazy population. In 2014, the percentage of Maine part-time workers who want more work but can't find it is the sixth highest of any state in the nation.

Even those Mainers who have found work are struggling to keep their heads above water in Maine's current economy. A report by the U.S. Bureau of Economic Analysis found that during 2011 and 2012, Mainers experienced the second-worst real income growth of any state in the country, with incomes increasing at just 0.3 percent.

A 2014 report on Maine's labor market by the Maine Center for Economic Policy shows that the gulf between the two Maines has also widened under LePage. The Portland, Bangor, and Lewiston metropolitan areas have garnered 83 percent of the total job growth under LePage, despite accounting for less than half the population of the state. Even compared with other states where unemployment is higher in rural areas, the disparity in Maine is one of the largest in the nation.

LePage's Maine may be open for business, but few are buying, and it has often been LePage's rural base that has been hit hardest by his economy.

chapter 14 Conclusion

The two qualities that Paul LePage's supporters might most readily identify with the governor are his authentic commitment to core beliefs and his willingness to pursue what they see as needed but sometimes controversial policies, regardless of the consequences or of who stands in his way. What LePage's conduct in office shows, however, is that these qualities, at their core, are based in insularity and pessimism.

LePage is insulated in terms of contact both with people and with ideas. He evaluates those around him and quickly decides whether they're with him or against him, rarely changing his mind. Supporters of his political, personal, and policy goals are given access and influence—sometime to unfortunate degrees—while those he sees as enemies are frozen out and attacked.

While this kind of sorting has always existed in politics to some degree, LePage and the Tea Party have raised it to a new level, demonizing and refusing to work in even the smallest ways with those they oppose. This propensity helps to explain why LePage refused to meet even briefly with elected Democratic leaders while at the same time spending hours meeting with and encouraging a group of anti-Semitic conspiracy theorists who accused those same leaders of treason and sought their execution. It's also the reason why, once they got a foot in the door of his campaign and transition, lobbyists were able to take over and run significant portions of his administration for the benefit of their corporate clients.

This black-and-white thinking is likely why LePage's initial promises of transparency were forgotten once he was exposed to an inquisitive public media, to be replaced with angry rants about newspapers and Freedom of Access laws.

This same insularity, on a more personal level, is spoken of with exasperation by some of LePage's own staff. Even some of his closest advisers feel they sometimes have less ability to influence his actions than Tea Party activists or right-wing radio hosts. They are often left cringing as he makes angry public statements or repeats right-wing conspiracy theories that undermine his credibility and harm his administration's agenda.

LePage has made some of his harshest attacks on those he thinks should be on his side but haven't shown absolute loyalty, such as when he has lashed out at Republican legislators for not fully supporting his agenda or attacked members of boards and commissions he himself has appointed for slowing his priorities.

LePage's insularity reached a ridiculous level when he threatened to move his office out of the State House completely. It also led in 2014 to the first time in modern Maine history that a budget bill was passed without any input from the governor, with LePage refusing to participate at all if his policies weren't adopted without question.

Perhaps it is LePage's insularity within Tea Party circles that has bred the deep-seated pessimism he obviously feels about the state he governs and its people. Almost all of his angry and incorrect public statements have this pessimism in common, whether it's claiming that Maine's schools are failing when they're actually among the best in the country, or when he falsely laments that 47 percent of able-bodied Mainers aren't working, despite Maine's high productivity and labor force participation rate.

This pessimism has led him to make strange claims about and pursue counterproductive policies on wind power and health care, and it has led him to vastly overstate welfare fraud and the supposed detrimental economic effects of environmental regulations.

In its most radical form, this pessimism has led LePage to believe and state publicly that the federal government has become the "new Gestapo" and, in private meetings, to discuss with conspiracy theorists what he will do if the federal government allows Russian troops to invade North America.

In some ways, this insularity and pessimism have led LePage to govern even more conservatively than he campaigned. Where he once promised compassion in public assistance, he now pursues only punitive measures. Where he once promised transparency, he now seeks to hide his words and actions from those he sees as political enemies. Where he once promised not to pick winners and losers and to create an "open for business" climate, he now holds up investments and targets companies based on ideology.

These two attributes and actions have made LePage a figure of national ridicule and a dangerous and unstable force in state politics. They have led him to make statements that denigrate Maine's people, schools, and economy and to pursue policies that are actively harmful to his state. Ironically, many of the economic and human costs have been borne by the demographic groups and geographic regions that most helped to elect him.

A Failed CEO

Just like his statements about Maine's students, buffaloes, and wind turbines, the central claim of LePage's governorship–that his policies have encouraged job creation and broad economic improvement–is demonstrably false. Chapters 9 (Taxes and Budgets), 12 (Labor), and 13 (Jobs) examine aspects of his record in this area in detail. Here in brief is a broader view. It relies heavily on information from the Maine Center for Economic Policy, which has charted the Maine economy for two decades and has delved into issues like wealth and income disparity long before they became prominent in the national consciousness.

Only wages for the highest income earners had been improving in the decade before LePage became governor. The rest of Maine hadn't yet recovered from the recession of 2001 by 2008. In fact, most workers earned lower inflation-adjusted wages in 2007 than in 2002

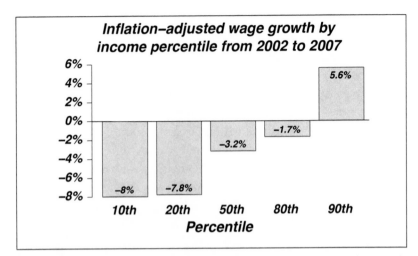

Figure 14.1. Only the top 10 percent of wage earners in Maine were earning more in 2007 than 2002. The rest were earning less on an inflation-adjusted basis. In other words, wages had failed to recover from the 2001 recession before the 2007 recession began. [Source: "The State of Working Maine in 2013," Maine Center for Economic Policy, November 2013, from Economic Policy Institute analysis of Current Population Survey, Outgoing Rotation Group]

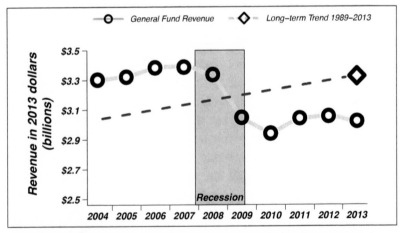

Figure 14.2. Maine's general-fund revenues plunged during the most recent recession and have not recovered. [Source: "Revenue Collapse Creates Budget Gap," Maine Center for Economic Policy, January 2013, from Maine Legislature, Office of Fiscal and Program Review]

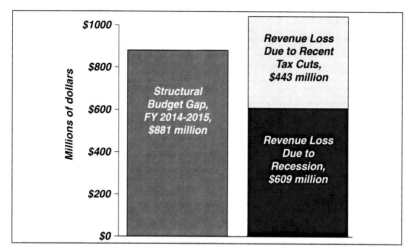

Figure 14.3. If not for the recession and tax cuts, the state would have enough revenue in the 2014–15 biennium to meet its obligations (including municipal revenue sharing), with money left over. [Source: "Revenue Collapse Creates Budget Gap," Maine Center for Economic Policy, January 2013, from Maine Legislature, Office of Fiscal and Program Review; and Maine Department of Administrative and Financial Services]

(Figure 14.1). The Great Recession of 2008 with its fresh round of job losses and foreclosures was therefore another blow to people who were already hurting. This protracted downturn and disparity created some of the resentment that LePage and the Tea Party capitalized on in the 2010 election.

LePage's response to this economic reality was to push cuts in income and estate taxes through the Republican-controlled legislature in 2011, his first year in office. Combined with the decreased state revenues Maine was already experiencing from the economic downturn, these unfunded tax cuts blew a hole in the state budget while providing little in terms of economic growth (Figures 14.2 and 14.3).

LePage's eventual response to the budget gap (as well as his answer to what he called a moral issue of people and towns depending too much on state funds) was to cut state programs and municipal revenue sharing. The 2012 compromise budget eventually included

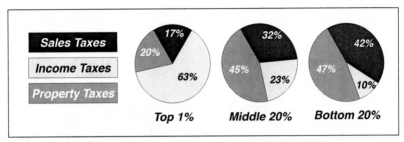

Figure 14.4. Property and sales taxes hit low- and middle-income taxpayers hardest, constituting 90 percent of the overall tax burden for low-income Mainers but only 37 percent for the wealthy. [Source: "The Consequences of Maine's Income Tax Cuts," Maine Center for Economic Policy, October 2012, *from* Maine Revenue Services Tax Incidence Study, 2009. *Note: Due to rounding, figures may not sum to 100%.]*

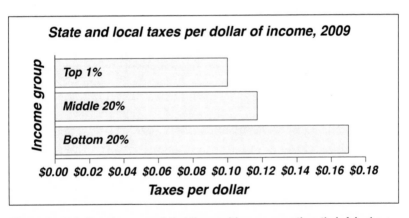

Figure 14.5. LePage has argued that the wealthy pay more than their fair share of taxes. The reality in Maine, even before his tax shifts, was that the bottom 20 percent of earners paid 17 cents of taxes for every dollar earned, whereas the top 1 percent paid 10 cents of taxes for every dollar of income. [Source: "The Consequences of Maine's Income Tax Cuts," Maine Center for Economic Policy, October 2012, from Maine Revenue Services Tax Incidence Study, 2009]

some of these provisions as well as increased sales taxes. The overall result has been a shift from the income tax–which is more progressive–to property and sales taxes–which are far more regressive (Figures 14.4 and 14.5). The overall impact of LePage's budgetary policies has therefore been a windfall for the wealthy but higher total taxes for low-income Mainers.

But it's worse than that. Rather than creating more job and income opportunities for all and merely aggravating income disparities as a secondary effect, LePage's tax cuts, spending cuts, and failure to invest in the state's future have significantly held back job growth in Maine. The state's recovery of jobs since 2008 has been slower than in any other postwar recession (Figure 14.6) and has lagged the rest of New England and the U.S. (Figure 14.7 and Table 14.1).

	Number of Jobs Lost Due to Recession (000s)	Number of Jobs Recovered (000s)	Percent of Lost Jobs Recovered
Maine	30.5	14.9	49%
New England	312.8	301.0	96%
United States	8,695	8,044	93%

Table 14.1. Through February 2014, Maine's recovery of jobs lost in the 2008 recession lagged New England and the U.S. [Source: "Maine's Labor Market Recovery: Far From Complete," by Joel Johnson and Garrett Martin, Maine Center for Economic Policy, April 2014, from MECEP analysis of U.S. Bureau of Labor Statistics, Current Employment Statistics Program data]

Indeed, data released on April 24, 2014, by the U.S. Bureau of Economic Analysis show that, in the 12-month period from 2011 to 2012, Maine ranked second-to-last among the fifty states, with per-capita personal income growth of 0.3 percent. Only South Dakota fared worse.

Given Maine's slow job recovery (Figure 14.8) and the state's ongoing shift from a manufacturing to a service economy (Figures 14.9 and 14.10), LePage's refusal to accept Medicaid funds from the federal government–funds that the Maine Center for Economic Policy has estimated would create 4,400 jobs in the state–seems misguided at best.

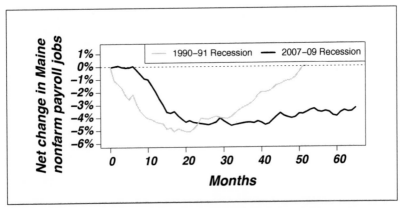

Figure 14.6. A comparison of Maine's net change in nonfarm jobs during and after the two deepest post-World War II recessions shows that the recovery of jobs since 2007 is even slower than after the recession of 1990–91. [Source: "The State of Working Maine in 2013," Maine Center for Economic Policy, November 2013, from the Maine Department of Labor]

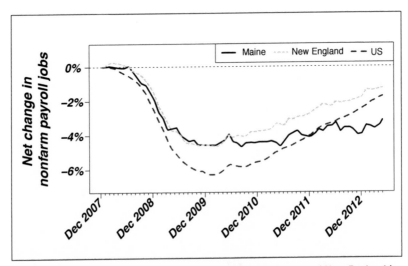

Figure 14.7. Job losses in Maine tracked closely with the rest of New England in 2008 and 2009, but Maine's recovery since 2010 has lagged New England and the U.S. [Source: "The State of Working Maine in 2013," Maine Center for Economic Policy, November 2013, from the U.S. Bureau of Labor Statistics and the Maine Department of Labor]

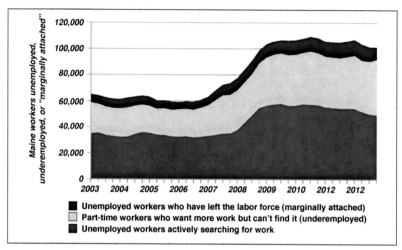

Figure 14.8. As of September 2013, more than 100,000 Maine workers were unemployed, underemployed, or marginally attached (i.e., unemployed workers who had abandoned the labor force). [Source: "The State of Working Maine in 2013," Maine Center for Economic Policy, November 2013, from the U.S. Bureau of Labor Statistics]

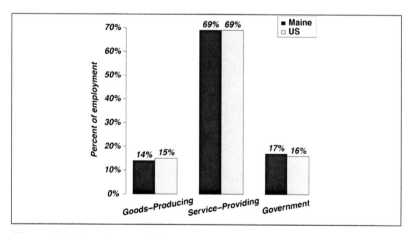

Figure 14.9. Through most of the twentieth century, a higher percentage of Maine's jobs were in manufacturing than in the rest of the U.S. Today, however, Maine's job distribution tracks closely with the rest of the country. [Source: "The State of Working Maine in 2013," Maine Center for Economic Policy, November 2013, from the U.S. Bureau of Labor Statistics, Quarterly Census of Employment and Wages]

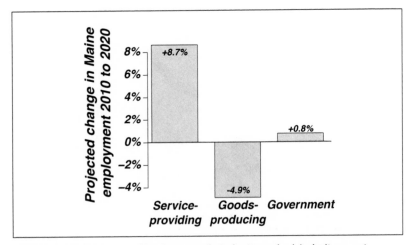

Figure 14.10. Maine's transition from manufacturing to service jobs isn't over yet. [Source: "The State of Working Maine in 2013," Maine Center for Economic Policy, November 2013, from MECEP analysis of Maine Department of Labor employment projections]

As mentioned in Chapter 13, nationwide employment finally surpassed its prerecession peak in May 2014, with 8.8 million more people working than in the February 2010 trough. Maine, however, has regained only about half of its 30,000 lost jobs. The difference has been three and a half years of Paul LePage as governor.

What's Next?

The looming question for Paul LePage's administration and for the Tea Party in general is whether the grassroots energy and hard-right ideology of the movement will have a lasting electoral effect in conservatives' favor in Maine and nationally, or if the primary and general election victories of 2010 will represent the high-water mark of a receding movement. Will the Tea Party be a cohesive force that can affect politics broadly or will it splinter and fade, maintaining influence only in Republican primaries–keeping candidates ideologically pure while damaging their chances in general elections?

Two statewide votes in Maine since LePage's 2010 victory may give some indication of an answer. In the referendum election in 2011, 61 percent of Maine voters rejected an attempt by Republicans to restrict voting rights, and in the 2012 general election, Democrats gained back control of both chambers of the state legislature.

During the first year of LePage's administration, the Republican-controlled Maine Legislature passed and the governor signed a bill to restrict voting rights, ending Maine's practice of allowing voters to register on election day at the polls. The move was part of a nationwide push to restrict voting rights backed by national conservative and corporate groups, including ALEC. Ostensibly meant to combat voter fraud, the bills submitted across the country to restrict voter eligibility and make registering and voting more onerous have the practical effect of reducing turnout among young, poor, and minority voters, demographics that skew Democratic.

Maine has a proud history of town-hall style democracy and of encouraging voter participation. In most recent national elections, the state has vied with Minnesota for the honor of having the highest rate of voter turnout of any state in the country. Maine was the first state to pass a law allowing voters to register on election day, and the provision had been in effect for 38 years with few complaints before Republicans passed the bill along party lines to repeal it. Another bill, which would have required photo identification at the polls, failed by a narrow margin.

While LePage supported and signed the 2011 legislation, the issue was one of the few conservative causes during his administration for which he wasn't the public face. The most visible backers of the bill were Secretary of State Charlie Summers (who would be the Republican nominee for U.S. Senate in 2012, losing to independent Angus King) and Maine GOP Chairman Charlie Webster.

Webster is a lot like LePage. Both are known for their bombastic personal styles, commitment to the conservative grassroots, and tendency to make controversial public statements. During the campaign, Webster made a series of what turned out to be unfounded claims about voter fraud, including accusations against students at

Maine colleges. Summers investigated Webster's allegations in his role as attorney general and, while he found no violations, nevertheless insisted that fraud was a serious concern and sent a letter to targeted students warning them about Maine's residency and vehicle registration laws. The American Civil Liberties Union deemed the letter "threatening" and "likely to deter them from exercising their voting rights."

After his side lost the election, Webster claimed that the referendum election was itself riddled with fraud. He garnered national headlines when he claimed as evidence that he had heard about "dozens of black people who came in to vote" in rural towns throughout the state and that "nobody in town knew them." Webster vowed to launch an investigation into these mysterious black people, but later backed down. The voting restrictions were rejected.

What won the election wasn't fraud but an outpouring of grassroots activism, in part triggered by LePage's first controversial year in office. When the law passed, a number of progressive organizations came together to form the Protect Maine Votes coalition, which launched a citizens' veto referendum and successfully gathered almost 70,000 signatures against the bill in less than a month in order to put it to a statewide vote. That level of interest and activism continued throughout the campaign and was a major factor in the landslide defeat of the controversial law.

Interestingly, the percentage of the vote in favor of keeping the voting restrictions was 39 percent, similar to the percentage LePage had won in his election as governor.

Protect Maine Votes outraised and outspent the GOP and the conservative groups in favor of the restriction thanks to large contributions from labor unions and from hedge-fund owner Donald Sussman, husband of Maine First Congressional District Representative Chellie Pingree. The main source of funding for the anti same-day registration side wasn't known until after the election was over. It was eventually revealed that 78 percent of the "No" side's funds ($250,000) came from an obscure Michigan-based group called the American Justice Partnership. AJP works closely with national organizations like ALEC and the Heritage Foundation and has the same mailing address as the Michigan Chamber of Commerce, the group that had surprised many by becoming involved in the 2010 gubernatorial election, giving $225,000 to boost LePage.

The 2012 general election was much more hotly contested than the 2011 referendum and, in a presidential year, saw much higher turnout, but the results were the same as in 2011. Republicans were again faced with an electorate energized by their opposition to LePage and GOP policies in Augusta and were once again handed a lopsided defeat.

While LePage's policies were front and center during the election, in which all the seats in the Maine House and Senate were up for grabs, the governor himself wasn't. He didn't do much stumping for Republican candidates and, except for one early TV ad targeting Republican senators, he also wasn't mentioned by Democrats or their progressive allies. The focus of campaign advertising was instead mostly on some of what LePage had attempted to portray as the major accomplishments of his administration, including income and estate tax cuts, health insurance reforms, and education initiatives.

The electorate apparently believed that the tax cuts primarily benefited the wealthy, the health care rate hikes benefited insurance companies, and the charter and private school legislation was more beneficial to for-profit education companies than to Maine children. Democrats won majorities in both houses, but not the two-thirds of seats needed to override LePage's vetoes. In the house, Republicans were reduced to 61 seats, 40 percent of the total. In the senate, they won only 15, 37 percent of the seats in the chamber. Again, these numbers are similar to LePage's 38 percent share of the vote in 2010.

Some of the same issues will likely be central to the 2014 election–in which LePage is attempting to win a second term–along with new ones such as the minimum wage, Medicaid expansion, LePage's job-creation record, and his reforms and cuts to public assistance programs.

While a percentage of the vote in the high thirties isn't enough to claim victory in a referendum or gain control of the legislature, it may again be enough for LePage to win a three-way race for governor. His

2014 opponents are Democratic Congressman Mike Michaud, a fellow Franco-American who has represented most of central and northern Maine in Congress for a decade, and Eliot Cutler, the wealthy independent who finished a close second to LePage in the 2010 election.

Because of the three-way race, it's certainly possible for LePage to win reelection despite his consistently low approval ratings. It may be less likely in 2014 than in 2010, as Michaud represents a stronger Democratic challenger than Libby Mitchell did, but if LePage's opponents once again split the vote and he is able to maintain his standing and motivate his base, 2014 could be a repeat of 2010.

Because of this dynamic, much of what LePage has done that might have been political suicide in a different state or if he were facing only a single opponent may actually rebound to his benefit. He doesn't need to build a broad coalition and convince more than 50 percent of the electorate; he need only maintain his 38 percent, make sure his supporters make it to the polls, and hope that his opponents both win enough of the vote to nullify each other. Polls during the first six months of the race confirm this effect, showing Michaud with perhaps just enough support to defeat LePage while Cutler wins enough moderate and progressive voters to keep the race up for grabs.

LePage, for all his flaws as a communicator, does an excellent job of speaking to elements of his base. A good example is his outreach to social conservatives and the religious right. LePage has taken no real substantive actions as governor on social issues like same-sex marriage and abortion rights. During the successful 2012 Maine equal marriage referendum, he remained publicly silent. Previously, during his campaign, he mostly avoided the subjects and seemed confused about what a civil union even was. He has proposed no new laws limiting the availability of abortion services. In one of his few relevant legislative actions, the veto of a bill to provide family planning coverage for low-income Mainers, the reason he listed for the veto was not that money would go to Planned Parenthood but instead that the law was duplicative and that women could seek coverage through the Affordable Care Act's health insurance exchange (ignoring, of course, that many of the state's poorest residents wouldn't be able to access care because of his previous veto of health care expansion). Current and former members of his staff readily confirm that social issues aren't on his radar.

Despite this, LePage has maintained the strong support of the religious right in Maine. A few key actions, like being the first governor in decades to attend and speak at an annual pro-life rally held at the State House, seem to have been enough to win their strong backing, with no need to take legislative action on their issues.

LePage, unlike most incumbents in a period of economic recovery, does not seem to have increased his approval ratings from when he first won office. A similar percentage to what he won in 2010, just less than 40 percent of the electorate, still express approval for his job as governor. This confirms an important fact about LePage and his administration: Even as his angry public statements, right-wing policies, and refusal to compromise may have driven some voters away, they have served to maintain and strengthen his standing among his Tea Party base.

LePage's insularity and pessimism may turn off swing voters and have led to policies that have been disastrous for the state, but they have served him well with his core supporters. For Tea Party voters, the controversy he constantly engenders is just a sign that he's shaking things up in Augusta. In many ways, his extreme statements and actions have inoculated him from charges that he has sold out and become just another politician and have helped to keep in his corner exactly the voters he needs to show up on Election Day to win reelection.

Perhaps because of LePage's actions, the Tea Party in Maine hasn't waned in the same way national polls show it may have in other parts of the country. While the movement may not be as visible as it was in 2010, the sentiment remains. Maine polls from the beginning of 2011 to the end of 2013 show a straight line of support, with just under 30 percent of Maine voters continuing to identify themselves as supporters of the Tea Party movement.

In the end, whether LePage continues in office and whether the Tea Party continues their influence in Maine's government may be determined not by broad political trends or the success or failure of particular policies, but by whether LePage's actions have galvanized moderate and progressive voters as much as they have his Tea Party partisans. Will they make it out to vote, and if they do, will they cast their ballots strategically for one of his opponents rather than splitting them between the two?

This may seem to be an electoral situation unique to Maine, but the same general political dynamic will determine the future of the Tea Party across the country. Will a motivated, conservative few continue to hold sway in low-turnout elections, or will a backlash by more moderate Republicans in primaries and among more progressive voters in general elections end their potency as a political force? Maine's next election may once again prove to be a bellwether.

Acknowledgments

In writing this book, I've relied on the knowledge and expertise of dozens of journalists, government staff, political operatives, and issue advocates from across the state of Maine. I'd especially like to thank the many current and former members of Governor LePage's campaign and administration who acted as sources both on and off the record. Their willingness to provide information and context despite our frequent differences of opinion on policy reflects the best aspects of the small, generally friendly world of Maine politics.

Thank you to Maine's political press corps, especially those few intrepid investigative journalists who have revealed important aspects of the LePage administration's actions despite stonewalling and accusations of bias. Their contributions can be found in nearly every chapter.

Thank you to my editors at the *Portland Press Herald* and *Bangor Daily News* who gave me the platforms to publish first takes on many of the parts that now make up this book. Writing those columns and blog posts and the feedback they prompted have made this a more collaborative and enjoyable project.

Thank you to my friends and colleagues at the Maine People's Alliance and the broader progressive movement in Maine who work every day to show the human impact of government policies, champion the best values of our community, and speak as the conscience of our state. I hope this book, in a small way, serves those same goals.

Jonathan Eaton, co-owner of Tilbury House Publishing, deserves special acknowledgment. Without him, this book wouldn't exist. The entire enterprise was his idea, and it was only his dogged insistence on deadlines that allowed the final result to be published in something approaching a timely manner. I hope I haven't strayed too far from his vision.

Finally and most importantly, thank you to my wife, who gave up many months of nights and weekends with her husband. She served as the main sounding board for the ideas expressed here and provided the love, encouragement, and emotional support that allowed me to complete this book and emerge relatively sane from listening to hundreds of hours of right-wing radio. I love you, Maggie.

About the Author

Mike Tipping is a columnist for the *Portland Press Herald* and the *Bangor Daily News* whose writing has brought to public light many of Governor LePage's most controversial statements and actions. He serves as communications director for the Maine People's Alliance and Maine People's Resource Center, two progressive nonprofit organizations dedicated to grassroots organizing and involving Maine people, especially from underrepresented groups, in civic life. His work for MPRC includes overseeing the state's most consistently accurate public opinion polling operation.

Mike grew up in Orono, Maine, and studied political science at Dalhousie University in Halifax, Nova Scotia, where he served as president of the Dalhousie Student Union and chair of the Alliance of Nova Scotia Student Associations. His brother, Ryan, represents their hometown in the Maine House of Representatives.

Mike lives in Westbrook, Maine, with his wife and two newborn sons.

CPSIA information can be obtained at www.ICGtesting.com
Printed in the USA
BVOW07s2242080714

358530BV00001B/2/P